NOW YOU WANT ME, NOW YOU DON'T!

Fear of Intimacy:
Ten ways to recognize it and ten ways to manage it in your relationship

Dr. Jeanette Raymond

Now You Want Me, Now You Don't!

Copyright © 2014 by Dr. Jeanette Raymond

All rights reserved. No part of this book may be reproduced or transmitted in any form or by any means without written permission of the author.

The characters in this book are fictitious and any resemblance to real individuals is purely coincidental.

ISBN 978-0-9915180-0-5

DEDICATION

I owe my inspiration to all the patients I have worked with over the last two decades. It has been a privilege to bear witness to your suffering and bravery as you struggled to gain the closeness with your partners that you so richly deserved. Helping you achieve the kind of emotional intimacy you craved has been immensely rewarding and prompted me to write this book, so that a wider audience can also benefit.

I want to express my heartfelt thanks to my mentor and editor, Jean-Noel Bassior, who believed that I had an important perspective to offer in the area of intimate relationships, and who patiently encouraged me to develop a writing style that brought life to the page. Her steadfast support and guidance every step of the way has been invaluable.

I am also indebted to my long-time friends Peter and Eiryl Wells from Wales, who read the first raw drafts of the book and gave me the courage to include my own experiences in the narrative.

CONTENTS

Introduction 1
1 The Ideal Marriage Becomes Torture 5
2 Couples Therapy Fails 9
3 Christy 15
4 Rick 21
5 Fear of Intimacy – Sign 1: Getting Busy 27
6 Christy 37
7 Rick 43
8 Fear of Intimacy – Sign 2: Complaining
   About Being Busy 49
9 Christy 59
10 Rick 63
11 Fear of Intimacy – Sign 3: Doing Good Deeds 67
12 Christy 79
13 Rick 83
14 Fear of Intimacy – Sign 4: Disgusted by
   Caring Remarks 87
15 Christy 97

16	Rick 101
17	Fear of Intimacy – Sign 5: Mistrusting Caring Actions. 105
18	Christy. 117
19	Rick 123
20	Fear of Intimacy – Sign 6: Discomfort at Receiving Compliments. 131
21	Christy. 143
22	Rick 147
23	Fear of Intimacy – Sign 7: Viewing Closeness as Parasitic. 153
24	Christy. 165
25	Rick 171
26	Fear of Intimacy – Sign 8: Getting Sick When Your Partner Misses You 175
27	Fear Of Intimacy – Sign 9: Dehumanizing Loved Ones 187
28	Fear of Intimacy – Sign 10: Using Anxiety to Keep Loved Ones at Bay. 199
29	Mourning the Past: Facing Intimacy Safely and Securely. 211
Afterword 215	

INTRODUCTION

"For love would be love of the wrong thing; there is yet faith, but the faith and the love and the hope are all in the waiting."

– T. S. Eliot

As a psychologist and psychotherapist, I've found that the commonly held notion that "the only thing men want is sex" and "the only thing women want is affection and talking" couldn't be further from the truth. Men long for emotional connection with their partners as much or even more than women do. In my experience, married men far outnumber women in wanting closeness with their spouses and often make that first call to the therapist's office when all else has failed. In fact, over the last ten years, ninety percent of the clients who sought me out for relationship problems involving emotional intimacy have been men.

Both men and women want to be the number one person in their partner's life. Each wants to be the light and heartbeat that excites and energizes their mate. Enjoying that special connection that includes sharing secrets, fears, fantasies and disappointments without fear of judgment is the essence of the emotional intimacy that couples crave. Often, each member tells me that relying on their partner to be emotionally available when they are stressed is at the top of their "relationship satisfaction" list. They want their partners to listen and join them in whatever emotional place they are in – not try to change or fix them.

When a man wants his partner to tune into his anxiety about work after a long, tough day, but instead gets a wonderful meal on the table, he may appreciate the meal but secretly feel that his stomach is more important to his spouse than his emotional well-being. His partner, on the other hand, may think that she's being caring when she anticipates his hunger and prepares his favorite food. She wants him to notice her thoughtfulness and desire to please, despite her frantic day, and is equally disappointed when her efforts are not met with enthusiasm. The ritual of perfunctory thanks and small talk that accompany the meal is a poor substitute for the deep emotional connection both were hoping for.

Women want their partners to zoom in on their sense of overwhelm, fear of inadequacy, and the exhaustion of juggling a sick child, a time-sensitive task at work, and preparing for a family birthday celebration. Flowers, eating out, or expensive gifts don't hit the spot where she needs to be seen, understood and attended to. These gifts are poor proxies for the focus and caring she craves from her partner. Her man, however, may believe he is easing her burden and expects his gifts to be comforting.

Introduction

Now You Love Me, Now You Don't tells the story of Rick and Christy who each yearned for emotional connection but failed in their efforts to meet each other's needs. Having come from family backgrounds where intimacy was shunned, neither had any clue as to how to read the other's attempts at closeness, and they could not relate intimately without fear getting in the way. Their marriage became lifeless and loveless – until Rick decided to do something about it. His desperation to get close to his wife and save his marriage made him reach out to me for couples therapy, and he was willing to attend counseling by himself when Christy walked out in the middle of the third session.

This book gives you a front row seat in the therapist's office, where you'll see first-hand how Rick's "push/pull" way of relating to me mirrored his marital experience. Again and again, I was challenged and disheartened as he pushed me away and devalued my efforts to nurture and support him, pulling me back in only when he wanted sympathy. Rick's stormy behavior impacted me personally and professionally, challenging me to remain steady and available, no matter how much he rocked the boat. There were many times when I thought he might sever our frail but hard-won ties as we came up against his rage and fear. But I fought for our relationship so that Rick could break through the barriers that were holding him back from being consistently intimate with his wife. Through our face-to-face interaction I taught him how to recognize, offer and accept intimate overtures that he had previously dismissed.

From Rick's detailed accounts, week after week, of his uphill struggle to create intimacy with Christy, I identified ten subtle signs of fear that his wife exhibited. Then I offered Rick ten strategies to help him make Christy feel safer, so that they could connect in ways that were mutually rewarding. The journey was hard, frustrating, and often made Rick want to give up. But he persevered, dealing with all the unfinished business of his childhood that got in the way of making a healthy, adult and intimate connection with his wife.

Whether you are a woman like Christy, who longs for emotional intimacy but is too afraid to allow it, or a man like Rick, who is frustrated in his efforts to get it, you will relate to the enormous challenges and struggles that both partners endure when emotional intimacy is missing in a marriage.

Now You Love Me, Now You Don't will give you a deeper understanding of your partner, whether you are the one seeking more intimacy or the one fending it off due to unbearable fear. As you hear the different tempos and melodies on both sides of these marital music sheets, you can use the strategies I shared with Rick to make your own relationship more equal, intimate and harmonious.

CHAPTER 1
THE IDEAL MARRIAGE BECOMES TORTURE

"Things are always different than what they might be... If you wait for them to change, you will never do anything."

– Henry James, *The Portrait of a Lady*

After four years of marriage, one son, and continued efforts to get close to his wife, Christy, thirty-year-old photographer Rick was heartbroken at being shut out and kept out emotionally, no matter how hard he tried to connect. While his twenty-eight-year-old partner was passionate in bed, often initiating sex and enjoying it, when it came to emotional intimacy, Christy wriggled her way out of Rick's advances as if he was a boa constrictor about to strangle and swallow her up.

Rick thought back to their dating days when Christy lit up as they talked about their mutual love of traveling and trying new foods. She glowed with excitement as they shared their vision of the kind of home and family life they wanted. They had so much in common and seemed to fit together so well that Rick knew they would always be best friends, loyal lovers and confidants, trusting each other with their wildest fantasies and deepest fears. Yet months after they said their "I dos," Rick just couldn't get his head around the fact that his warm but shy bride, who was sexually voracious in bed, had morphed into a stern, cold robot outside their love-making moments.

Seven months after the wedding, Rick began to feel as if his world was collapsing. He felt like an ant being trampled on each time he reached out to invite Christy to share his excitement about a new photography commission or his frustration about missing his favorite football game. She scolded him when he tried to check in with her during the day, as if his calls and text messages were frivolous interferences in her strictly-ordered and more legitimate schedule.

Rick recalled that just a couple of months into the marriage, it seemed that Christy got up each morning armed with a plan to brush off his invitations for connection. For every way he reached out to her for emotional intimacy, she had a well-rehearsed, justifiable reason why she couldn't respond. For weeks after the honeymoon, Rick thought it was just a phase his bride was going through, so he tried to recreate the magic of their courting days, hoping to find his loving and joyful woman again. But her mocking and dismissive responses made him feel small and ashamed for wanting to be close to his wife.

Rick tried to get onto Christy's radar by doing chores and taking care of both house and car repairs, as well as romancing her with flowers, dinners and spa getaways. But instead of treating him like a lover, Christy

The Ideal Marriage Becomes Torture

acknowledged his efforts as if he were a child who'd completed his math homework.

Still unwilling to admit that his wife had changed, Rick organized long weekends away, hoping to rekindle the closeness they'd had while dating. But Christy was outraged about the cost. She refused to take time off from her housekeeping duties and family obligations, accusing Rick of putting pressure on her to act irresponsibly.

As their second wedding anniversary approached, Rick was worried. He had a great relationship with their one-year-old son, Joel, but his marriage felt like a war zone where he fought valiantly each day, only to retreat at night, wounded and worn out. The chances of penetrating Christy's emotional fortress were little to none, and Rick was fast losing the will to fight for his right to have emotional intimacy with his wife.

Now, as they started their third year of marriage, Rick was forced to acknowledge his heartache and loneliness. His efforts to get emotionally close to Christy had failed miserably, so he turned the spotlight on himself. Was it his fault? Had he done something irreparable? He pleaded with Christy to tell him why she was shutting him out, but she denied doing any such thing and suggested he was going crazy. He wracked his brain, trying to figure out how things between them could have gone so wrong. Had he been blind when he was dating? Had he missed significant warning signs? Had he been fooled? Had she pretended to be someone she wasn't to reel him in? Was the person he fell in love with just an illusion?

For the next two years, Rick soldiered on, trying to be the dutiful husband. He decided to let the close bond he had with Joel compensate for the lack of emotional intimacy with Christy, but it didn't work. He still yearned for the excitement and energy he'd felt in Christy's presence during their courting days. Falling into a depression helped him numb his pain and longing, but as the fourth anniversary of their wedding approached, a volcano of rage rose up inside him threatening to destroy the marriage.

Rick felt so enraged at being robbed of the woman he thought he had married that he wanted vengeance – and what better way than cheating on her? An image of Christy betrayed and writhing in helpless agony when she discovered his affair gave him pleasure, making him feel like he had the upper hand. Yet ten minutes later, his stomach was in knots as anxiety about her reaction washed over him. What if she stopped sleeping with him? That was the one and only way he still could connect with her, and not something he was willing to risk. And what if she just cut the cord and filed for divorce? Not being able to see her or sleep beside her scared him more than anything. Cheating didn't seem like such a good idea when he imagined losing his wife altogether.

Rick had hit the wall and knew he had to take drastic measures. If he didn't act now, his marriage would disintegrate – and that's when I got his desperate call for marriage counseling. He was willing to do anything to save his marriage and begged Christy to come with him. She agreed, looking forward to showing me what a saint she was for putting up with her childish and irresponsible husband.

CHAPTER 2
COUPLES THERAPY FAILS

"The voyage of discovery is not in seeking new landscapes, but in having new eyes."

– Marcel Proust

"I can't take any more of this!" Christy said defiantly, as she grabbed her purse and walked out half-way through the third session of couples therapy. "He's the one with the problem, not me!" she huffed, slamming the door behind her.

Rick was hunched over, clasping and unclasping his hands, then rubbing his head as if he were totally lost. After about thirty seconds he looked at me, raised his eyebrows and shrugged his shoulders, hoping I would rescue him.

"You seem shocked and bruised. What's going on for you right now?" I asked, as Christy's accusatory voice reverberated in my throbbing head.

"I don't know," Rick said, his voice choked with sadness.

"Sounds like you feel the rug has been pulled from under you."

He nodded before saying, "Well, I guess that's it!" as he tried to stop himself from breaking down.

Just as he rose to follow his wife out the door, I said pointedly, "If you leave now, then you're giving up on yourself and your marriage, just like Christy did."

Shocked and speechless, he sat back on the couch and stared at me. I stared right back until he cried – deep, wracking sobs that shook his entire body as he tried to cover his face and keep the tears from falling on his jacket. I found myself tearing up too, sensing the pain he must be feeling as he tried to contain his utter dejection and loss of hope.

As Rick's gasps for air became more spaced out and he resumed his normal breathing, he mumbled, "Why shouldn't I give up? Why do *I* always have to be the one to keep things going?"

I dabbed at my own wet eyes, relieved that he wasn't going to amputate our relationship before we had made any headway.

"It's understandable that you are angry at having to carry the burden yourself. But the pain I heard when you cried tells me that your marriage means a great deal to you, and that you want to make it work."

"I've been in pain all my life, so what's new?" he said sarcastically, doing up a shirt button that had come undone, revealing a patch of black, hairy chest.

"The pain is familiar to you – maybe even part of your identity – but I sense that you know it's not natural. I think you want to ease the pain and feel cared for and loved for who you are, just like everyone else."

His lips curled up in a grimace of a smile as he shot a glance at me and then stared out the window. His chest heaved with deep breaths, as if he were trying to control himself. I felt that he'd slipped into another world where he was weighing his options, excluding me from the process. I waited anxiously to see whether he would let me be a source of comfort and support, or whether he would dismiss me as irrelevant, just as he seemed to be doing with his marriage.

"There's no point!" he said finally, making a move to get up and leave again.

"So you want to be like Christy?" I challenged. "Just give up and go back to a hurtful and lonely marriage?"

"I've already done everything I can," he shot back. "I've tried for the last four years, but things just get worse. I don't see how coming here for therapy on my own is going to make things any different."

"It's incredibly hard to work on a relationship when you feel alone and when you are in so much constant pain," I said gently. "Coming to therapy can help ease the pain and allow you to feel cared for."

He pulled his shoulders up, tidied his shirt and jacket, and told me that he didn't need consoling or comforting. He said that the only purpose he could see for therapy was to find ways of connecting with his wife and making her want to be close to him. But since he had already tried everything known to man, it was a fruitless exercise.

"You want my help in getting emotionally close to Christy, but you doubt that I have anything to offer that you haven't already tried," I said.

A hint of a smile crossed his face as he felt perfectly understood, and I grabbed the chance to show him that all was not lost.

"My guess is that you haven't focused on trying to understand what she is afraid of and what prevents her from being emotionally intimate with you on a consistent basis," I told him.

Rick's eyes widened. For a split second he seemed open and hopeful. Then a film came over his eyes and his facial expression became inscrutable, as if he was trying to avoid temptation.

"I don't see how that's going to help. I can't solve her problems," he said.

"Actually, you can!" I threw out the bait.

"What do you mean?" he asked quickly.

"If you know what her fears are and how they came to be there, you can use the strategies I suggest to help calm those fears, so she can be more available to you emotionally."

"But how can I do that if she won't come to therapy? How will I find out what she is afraid of?" he asked.

"Do you remember that I met with both you and Christy individually before this session to get a picture of your backgrounds? That information helped me to understand the emotional traumas both of you experienced, and from that I can gauge what gets triggered and replayed in your marriage."

"Oh! That sounds scary but exciting."

"What's the scary part?"

"I don't want to relive my past and have all that stuff stirred up."

"It's already getting stirred up every time you try to get emotionally intimate with Christy and you get blocked."

He looked at me suspiciously, so I asked, "And what's the exciting part?"

"I really like the idea of figuring out what's going on inside her and where it's coming from. When you told me her fear of closeness was coming from her early experiences, I felt taken off the hook, like it's not my fault."

"That's right. It's nobody's fault that you each have had your fair share of stress and emotional trauma growing up. But you can lessen its impact by understanding it and giving it less power."

Rick looked visibly relieved. He was opening up to me, and I took the opportunity to give him more incentives. "In addition, when you share your day-to-day experiences with Christy, I can help you see how the echoes from both your pasts tangle you up now, making you go round in exhausting circles. Then we'll work to find new ways you can use to counter her fears and manage your own anger and disappointment."

Rick perked up. He looked hopeful for the first time in this session. It was as if he was allowing himself to grasp a helping hand and trust it, rather than being the lonely, brave, suffering hero. He agreed to start weekly therapy sessions beginning the following Monday in November.

CHAPTER 3
CHRISTY

*"What is your substance, whereof are you made,
That millions of strange shadows on you tend?"*

– Shakespeare's Sonnets, LIII.

At the age of eighteen-and-a-half, Christy left her home in Los Angeles and set out for Taos, New Mexico, determined to prove to herself that she didn't need her mother's approval or her father to champion her dreams to be independent and make something of herself in the world.

The freedom to put herself first and not worry about her mother's mood swings or her father blowing hot and cold was exhilarating. She got a job in a beauty salon and enjoyed assisting the stylists. Customers actually noticed her and included her in their small talk. At times, she wanted to tell her parents about her adventures, hoping they would beg her to return and help her pursue her college dream. But the vision faded almost as soon as she created it, giving way to the memory that they didn't care a scrap when she left without telling them. They hadn't even tried to come after her or make sure she was okay.

Two weeks later, when she couldn't contain her desire to find out if they missed her or regretted not taking her aspirations seriously, she called and told them where she was. But it was less than five minutes before Sonia, her thirty-nine-year-old mother, an event planner, blamed Christy for causing her migraines and insomnia. Mark, her forty-year-old father, was, as usual, consumed with caring for his wife, leaving Christy feeling stuffed with her mother's woes and guilty for triggering them. And her father's consistent focus on his wife's moods rang a dull, hollow bell of emptiness inside her.

Each day she went to work hoping to be useful, appreciated and valued. But most of the time she was swamped with stuff to do for the many stylists, who all had different demands. Often she felt so bombarded with jobs that all needed to be done at the same time that she would try to make herself invisible to damp down their irritation and impatience with her delivery. It was a familiar feeling – exactly how she had protected herself as a child when her mother yelled at her to tidy up, help with the meals, and clean her room. It was always a family battle for who got to be "big" and alive, and who had to shrink, giving up their right to exist.

Becoming a machine was one of the ways Christy survived her mother's unsettled and cranky moods. She did everything Sonia ordered, often over and over again until she calmed down and left Christy alone. Having her life's blood sucked out by her mother's voracious needs made

Christy

her long for a smile or a hug – something that made her feel loved again – but it rarely came. It was hard for her to manage those awful feelings of being crammed to the gills with her mother's strange and scary emotions, and then being left alone with a gaping hole in her heart that she had no idea how to fill.

Other times, Christy would run away from her mother's bad moods. She would lock herself in her room and be totally silent. At times, she was scared that her mother would break down the door and obliterate her with her anxiety and frustrations; other times, she gloated when Sonia begged her to come out, apologizing, professing her love, and tempting her with her favorite foods. She steeled herself against the longing to rush into her mother's arms and be embraced with love. She knew that if she gave into that urge, she would be punished for putting Sonia through such an ordeal.

The hunger pangs she endured, barricaded in her room, were nothing compared to the thrill she got by ignoring her mother. In that isolation, she filled herself up with power and control and became invincible. Now her mother was the hungry one, needing her, begging *her* for forgiveness. Christy would emerge from her room much later, when it was time for her father to come home, knowing that her mother would brighten up, forgetting to give her the third degree for being denied entry into the bedroom.

Christy's heart beat faster as she anticipated her father's hug when he came home each evening from his investment banking job. He'd always be glad to see her and her sister, and he'd muss their hair and smile when they ran to him. Sometimes he put Christy on his lap and looked at her drawings, making her feel safe, loved and wanted. But his eyes soon shifted towards his wife, his ears tuning into her complaints about her day and how difficult Christy had been. Then she would feel her father's body tense up and leave her, replacing her with her mother.

Those icy moments of abandonment made Christy feel betrayed and lonely. But then her father would come back and want to get connected again. He would entice Christy to go for a walk, help him in the vegetable garden, or play checkers. The joy of being singled out as "Daddy's girl" – even for a just a few minutes – was the most seductive experience Christy had ever known.

But when they were together, her dad seemed down and absent, compelling Christy to bring him back to life by cheering him up. He'd respond for a little while, but as soon as they rejoined the family, she felt as if she had lost him again. Her sense of defeat made her hate the fact that, once again, she'd bought into his warm and charming invitation to be together. By the time she started first grade, she was guarded around her dad whenever he was inviting and affectionate. At those moments, she would imagine herself in a cocoon where she could feel his caress and hear his loving voice but be protected against the moment when he would turn away and abandon her.

At night, alone in her room when everyone else was sound asleep, Christy came out of her cocoon and touched herself in her private parts. It was comforting and electrifying, but most of all, she was in control of giving herself pleasure and attention. This nightly ritual gave her a refuge from the uncertainties of her mother's moods and availability and her father's tantalizing ways. She could hug and please herself for as long as she could stay awake, and she didn't have to share this with anyone, or guard it from her greedy mother.

Then, at age seven, she got left behind at the petting zoo during a family outing to the state fair and nearly died of shock, heartbreak and sheer terror. They'd been looking at the donkeys, goats and rabbits, and Christy was fascinated by one of the baby goats and trying to feed it, oblivious to the fact that her parents and sister, Sarah, had moved on. By the time she came out of her bubble, they were nowhere in sight.

She looked around frantically, helpless to control the tears of anguish that gushed down her face, wetting her hair and her tank top. Calling out to her mom and dad was like spitting in the wind – and she was furious! How could they so easily have forgotten her? Then fury gave way to despair, as the seconds and minutes ticked by with no sign of her parents. Maybe they wanted to get rid of her. Yes, that was it. They preferred her sister anyway, so they must have been planning to abandon her and run away with Sarah. After all, her mother was always saying what a handful she was and how ashamed she felt of her in public.

Christy's mind now spiraled out of control. What if they regretted having her? Her mother was always threatening to give her away and then claiming it was just a "joke." And her father often told her how tired he was when she tried to engage him in play. Had she worn him out? These fears escalated during the interminable minutes, which grew to hours, when she felt orphaned and abandoned forever. Now she was certain her parents had deserted her for being a "bad girl." Her anxieties were reinforced by punishing flashbacks to times when her mother had told her she was too "forward" and needed to be grateful for what she had, instead of wanting more.

Sobbing uncontrollably, Christy buried her face in the soft grass and thought of all the ways she could repent for her sins, hoping and praying that her parents would change their minds and rush back to rescue her. Would she be reclaimed as their precious daughter? Or would she be discarded like an empty candy wrapper in the overflowing trash bins of the zoo?

CHAPTER 4
RICK

"Only during hard times do people come to understand how difficult it is to be master of their feelings and thoughts."

– Anton Chekov

A month before he graduated from high school, eighteen-year-old Rick refused the invitation to attend his father's wedding in Tucson to Wendy, his longtime mistress. He was determined not to acknowledge this abomination of a liaison, coming just over a year after his parents' divorce. He hated his forty-five-year-old father, Jerry, for leaving him, his mother, and his younger sister, Beth, four years ago, and hadn't spoken to his father since. He ignored the encouragement he got from his forty-two-year-old mother, Angela, to go to the wedding and viewed thirteen-year-old Beth as a traitor for maintaining contact with their dad and taking part in the marriage ceremony.

Rick couldn't understand how his mother could accept the fact that her husband had cheated on her for years before divorcing her fourteen months ago. He hadn't forgiven his father for pretending to go out and play cards with friends after countless family evening meals, then coming home smelling of booze and perfume until the day he announced that he was leaving to move in with Wendy.

He was angry at his mother for her denial. Now she was saying that she'd been aware of her husband's cheating all along and denying that it had upset her. She was even pushing him to pretend that his father hadn't made her cry herself to sleep those many nights when he'd stayed up to make sure she was all right. How could she want him to deny the hundreds of loud and scary arguments he'd heard most weekends, when his mother would plan family activities and his father would use his real estate broker job as an excuse to avoid them? Was he also supposed to erase his desperate attempts to shield Beth from the violence in their parents' voices, while he could hardly manage his own fears? Did she really want him to forget how she'd disguised her exhaustion when she got home from her job as a hospice nurse, and how hard she'd tried to show interest in their homework and extra-curricular activities and tend to their childhood illnesses?

Rick bit his tongue and grit his teeth when his mother talked about the importance of him having a relationship with his father, rather than being loyal to her. His blood boiled as he recalled the constant terror he'd felt that his mother would get sick or die from stress if he failed to protect her by hiding his knowledge of his father's latest affair. To discover now that she'd known all along and had let her husband get away with it was mindboggling.

Rick

Well, *she* may have forgiven him and given up trying to make him take their marriage seriously, but *he* wasn't about to do any such thing. Jerry needed to be punished, and since neither his mother nor his sister was willing to do it, Rick felt he had to honor the family by snubbing his father.

Clearly, Beth was a traitor for siding with Jerry, especially since it was he who'd stepped in to save her from bullies at school and taken her to violin lessons when his mother had to work. He felt the bitter taste of vitriol as he remembered comforting his sister when their father failed to turn up at her games and concerts. He recalled how he'd buried his own disappointment at not having a chance to go camping with his dad more than once in his boyhood. He had lived in hope for those times when father and son would explore the world and come back with a wonderful bond that made him feel special, strong, and proud to be the eldest in the family. But plans were forgotten and promises broken, making him feel unwanted and unimportant to the most significant figure in his life.

In his final year at elementary school, when he first discovered his father's duplicity, Rick shouldered the role of husband and father himself. He did all the things he thought his father ought to do and wasn't doing, including trying to cheer his mother and encourage his sister to do well in school. He thought that if he stood tall and took up the slack, his father would be shamed into coming back and doing the job he had signed up for. But as the years passed, a slow-burning rage built up inside him as he realized that his father had no intention of changing his ways.

So Rick switched tactics and focused on his mother, trying to make up for her sadness and anxiety. He wanted to be the one to fill her up with life after his father had sapped the last drop of juice out of her frail and weakened emotional state. He became her escort, taking her to church, school and family events whenever his father was absent.

He couldn't understand why his mother didn't relish the fact that he was there whenever she needed him. He'd set himself up as her pillar of strength and fidelity, but she treated him as a mere child who couldn't possibly fulfill her as his father once had, and should. A nagging sense of failure stalked him in his quest to rescue his mother, and he often went to sleep planning ways to try harder so that he would be "good enough" for her.

Rick spent many a sleepless night for the remainder of his time at elementary school, bearing silent witness to his father's blatant double life. The scariest times came when his parents actually fought, rather than passing each other like ships in the night. His father usually drank all night, having run out of credible excuses to leave the house. Once a fight started, Rick knew it would go on for at least 40 minutes, so he'd play video games with his headphones on, trying to drown out the horror of the words flying between his parents. He wanted to burst into their bedroom and tell them both to grow up, "behave," and think about their kids. But he was scared that his father would laugh at him and his mother would simply dismiss him by telling him to get back to bed.

Rick

One night in particular still reverberated in his memory, shaking him up whenever he thought about it. His father had been more attentive to his mother recently, promising to be more involved in family affairs and activities. Angela had brightened, as she and her husband went out on 'dates' to revive their marriage. On this night, Rick was babysitting ten-year-old Beth, relieved that his parents were out showing the world that they were still a pair. But as the night wore on and they did not return, he became increasingly anxious and angry. By midnight, there was still no sign of them.

At first, he imagined that they were having a great time and didn't want to end the evening. By 2:00 a.m., he was irritated because they hadn't called and he didn't know where to reach them. At 4:00 a.m., he was frantic with worry. He didn't know who to contact at that hour. His mind jumped from the possibility of being orphaned by the death of his parents in a car crash to a vision of his mother ill in the hospital, abandoned yet again by his drunken, irresponsible dad. He even thought that his parents had run away together to start a new life away from their children, who were just nuisances, draining their exuberance and freedom.

His mind kept switching from the relief of not having to put up with his messy parents if they never turned up again, to the relief of knowing that he still had parents, no matter how awful they were. As dawn was about to break, his anxiety reached panic proportions. He was dizzy, sweaty and antsy. As he gasped for breath, he thought he was going to die.

CHAPTER 5
FEAR OF INTIMACY – SIGN 1: GETTING BUSY

"For pain must enter into its glorified life of memory before it can turn into compassion."

– George Elliot, *Middlemarch*

Memories of my parents' divorce when I was twelve came flooding back after Rick's first therapy session in late November. We both had a fierce sense of loyalty towards the parent who had been cheated on; in Rick's case, it was his mother, and for me, it was my father. We had both emerged from our childhoods wanting to compensate for those difficult times. Rick wanted to avoid a broken marriage at all costs, and I wanted to help people like him develop the foundation they needed to do just that.

As a young adult, I had wanted to "do it right" when it came to choosing a partner and settling down. I bent over backwards to make things work out in my romantic relationships, but felt my partners would sooner or later prefer someone else, which is exactly what happened. I read every psychology book on relationships and personalities, but none of it helped – until I went into therapy. My fear of being unworthy was eased by the relationship I formed with my therapist, who made me feel secure and cared for. When I later became a therapist myself, I became fascinated with the subtle ways in which people avoided emotional closeness and the fears that made them do so. I developed an expertise in sensing when one person reached out for closeness and the other one ran away.

In my twenty-fifth year as a psychotherapist, I had a real challenge on my hands with Rick. Would I be able to get him to a point where he could be more in tune with his wife, or would he just grow as an individual and become estranged from his spouse?

As he entered my office for his second session, his loneliness and degradation was palpable. I listened quietly as he poured out his sense of failure and hopelessness, trying to relate to Christy when she put him off with her busy schedule. He was particularly upset about an incident that had happened just a few days ago…

As soon as Rick put his key in the door at six o'clock on Wednesday night, he heard Christy chiding Joel while preparing dinner. She brushed off Rick's affectionate greeting, complaining that she had laundry to finish and Joel to bathe before they ate. Joel's delighted smile on seeing his father made up for the rejection, and after dinner, Rick tried again to connect with his wife. But she rattled off twenty things she had yet to do before the day was over.

For the second time that night, Rick swallowed his disappointment and frustration, intent on breaking down Christy's wall. At 10:30 p.m., he watched her going into the bathroom to brush her teeth – and that's when he decided to advance. He tried to approach her from a sympathetic place, but she suddenly remembered that she needed to put out clean towels, iron his shirt for the next day, and fill online orders from the Far East for her handmade knitted sweaters business.

Blocked for the third time that night, Rick finally lost his patience, accusing her of ignoring him and caring more about petty housekeeping routines than him. Christy fired back that he was behaving like a spoiled brat, ungrateful for all the chores she undertook on his behalf.

Stung with shame, Rick went to bed, turning away from her when she got in. Within a couple of minutes he felt her arms reaching for him as she thrust her body right up against him. Fueled with revenge, he pinned her arms down, smashed his lips against her neck, pushed his knees against her groin and penetrated her over and over again. He wanted to make her orgasm several times, so she was at his mercy. He finally stopped when his body hurt and Christy stiffened against him. A wave of tenderness came over him after his need to control her had been sated. He caressed her hair and her back, but she told him to stop because she had tons of things to do the next day and needed to sleep.

Now You Want Me, Now You Don't!

******

Rick's lips twisted with bitterness as he sat back and looked at me for a response.

"What was it like when she wanted you sexually?" I asked.

"She is like Jekyll and Hyde – a perfect robot who tackles endless jobs by day, and a ravenous lover by night!"

"I was interested in you, but you focused on Christy."

"I was explaining what it's like to be with her!" he replied indignantly.

"You say you want to be acknowledged, but when I asked about your feelings, you put the spotlight on Christy."

"It's embarrassing!"

"You felt a bit scared when I tried to get close to you just now. Perhaps Christy is also scared when you try to get close to her. You change the subject, while she hides behind her busy routine."

"So she comes out of hiding in bed?" he asked.

"Not quite. She hides behind her seductiveness."

"How do you know?" he challenged me.

"You can't see her vulnerability when she turns on her sexuality and doesn't have to see or care about your feelings."

Rick looked down and started to dust something off his blue jeans. A tiny muscle twitched just above his lip.

"It hurts to think that your feelings don't count, doesn't it?" I commented.

He nodded, avoiding eye contact with me.

Sign 1: Getting Busy

"It's like your parents not caring about your feelings when they argued and fought."

"Yes!" he said, letting out a huge sigh and settling back on a cushion. "I try to be affectionate and caring when I see how overloaded she is, but she pushes me aside."

"When Christy grabs you in bed, it's as if she's only interested in taking care of her needs, not *yours*."

"Yes! Why should I have to wait for her to be in the mood and then be there just at the moment she wants me?"

"You got back at her by taking charge of the sex between you."

"I was tired of being at the mercy of her whims," he snarled.

"Hold onto that feeling, and let's put Christy back in the picture. She was subject to her father's whims when she was a child. One minute she was his angel, and the next he'd ignore her," I pointed out. "She couldn't trust her father to be consistent, and now she can't trust you to be reliable either."

"I understand that she didn't have the best childhood," Rick said, leaning forward. But why do I get attacked just for trying to be on her radar?"

"Right now, she isn't sure if your understanding or sympathy is real or lasting. She needs her many tasks to act as a shield between the two of you, so she doesn't get seduced by your kindness," I explained.

"That sounds fucked up!" he said contemptuously.

"I wonder how you felt when your dad lied about where he was and who he was with. Did you trust him after that, even though he seemed loving and sincere?"

"No, of course not!" Rick yelled.

"Right. Well, Christy is in the same place you were in then. She doesn't trust that family members are what they seem to be on a consistent basis – and *you* are now family."

He was speechless.

"She wants to be in control, so there is no chance of you letting her down," I added.

I suggested to Rick that he might feel less rejected if he held onto the fact that they were both equally scared and unsure of each other, and that working on making the emotional climate safer would be a good first step in developing intimacy.

"Since Christy is busy much of the time, you could try joining her in household chores and in taking care of Joel's stuff," I offered. "If you fold laundry together, put away groceries or tidy up the bedroom, you are giving her the message that you want to share, but without intruding."

"I'm not sure how that will work. She may think I'm getting in the way and get even more irritated," Rick interjected.

"She might. But it's less likely if you do it casually, just kind of picking up the rhythm of the activity alongside her, and talking with her about your feelings in that moment."

"What do you mean by 'talking about my feelings in that moment'?"

"Let's say you are putting away groceries, and you notice that one of the items is bread. You can talk to her about your favorite sandwiches, the different kinds of bread you like, and so on. You start up a conversation that she can enter without the threat of feeling poked or exposed."

"It feels like you're making us strangers instead of intimate partners!" he said.

"So you want to achieve closeness all in one go?" I countered.

He raised his eyebrows and said softly, "I have been waiting a long time."

"Waiting is frustrating, but until she feels safe, she won't be able to respond to you."

"I get it, but it doesn't feel like it will ever happen," he said.

"Just as you join her in the tasks, she will join you in a spontaneous dialogue – and that becomes a moment of shared intimacy."

"But what if she says that she hasn't got time for chit-chat?" Rick asked.

"If you imagine being side by side with her, rather than entwined, she won't feel pressured," I said, hoping he'd give it a chance.

"Hmmm..." he murmured.

"I can tell you aren't sold on the idea, so maybe you won't be interested in the second part of this plan."

He stuck his hands in his jeans pockets and said unconvincingly: "I am interested."

"That sounds as if you *think* you should be interested, when what you really want is for me to show you how to make her comply with your expectations."

That sent him into a tailspin. He complained loudly about having to trust me and my suggestions, but after venting for several minutes, he calmed down and asked for the next part of the plan.

"Share some memories with your wife while you are doing chores together. Let's say you are tidying up Joel's toys and you find a broken action figure. That may remind you of what you liked to play with at Joel's age, and what it was like for you if any of your toys got broken. You could share that memory."

"What's that got to do with anything we are going through now?" Rick asked, clearly frustrated. I felt his wall going up, resisting my ideas.

"You felt better when I understood your experience of your parents fighting and not caring about you. Christy will be able to do the same when you share those childhood memories, bringing you closer."

"Why do we have to connect through bad memories?" he asked, looking sad.

"You had many rough times in your childhood, same as Christy. Sharing memories of those experiences will illuminate what you have in common and give you points of connection that you can build on."

A hint of a smirk crossed his lips as he commented, "It makes me feel like I've married a messed-up, broken woman."

"How would you like it to be when you share memories?"

"Like the times when my parents and I had fun together, before my mother got pregnant."

"Recreating those idyllic times with Christy may be attractive, but that excludes *her* history. How about creating new memories with her, using your past experiences as a sort of modeling clay?" I offered.

He picked up his jacket as the session came to an end and left, clearly upset that I was encouraging him to change course. I had an awful feeling that he was determined to make Christy bow to his will by trying to kill her with kindness or please her sexually. How could I help him feel safe enough to explore Christy's past and disclose his, when he was adamant about following a route towards intimacy that had already failed?

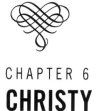

CHAPTER 6
CHRISTY

"Those better sorrows of childhood! When sorrow is all new and strange, when hope has not yet got wings to fly beyond the days and weeks, and the space from summer to summer seems measureless."

– George Elliot, *The Mill on the Floss*

Fervent praying and resolve to be a "good girl" finally brought Christy's family back to her at the petting zoo after what seemed like an eternity. The immense relief that washed over her whole body at the sight of them stifled her wish to beat them black and blue for daring to forget her.

Her mother was angry at her for not paying attention and making them waste two hours looking for her. Her father seemed happy to see her, though he didn't say anything. He just told her to get a move on because they would be late for supper at Aunt Margaret's place. It was only five-year-old Sarah who held her hand, quietly welcoming her back into the fold.

The journey to and from her aunt's house was a blur. All Christy could think was, *How could they not notice? Didn't they feel the world shake under their feet when I was missing from their side?* She threw up at Aunt Margaret's place and felt her mother's hands cleaning her up and brushing her hair. Her mother's touch felt soothing on her skin, but there were no words of comfort or love, leaving her insides raw and hemorrhaging. Her mother seemed repulsed by her vomit and embarrassed at having to attend to it.

For the rest of the day, as she recovered from this emotional trauma, Christy felt the futility of yearning for tenderness, concern and comfort from her parents. The longing to be tuned in to and cared for was now an enemy she had to defend against. She noticed that when Sonia was disgusted by her behavior, she had no warm feelings for her daughter. It was as if the disgust severed the mother-daughter connection altogether. So what better role model to use than her own mother? Christy switched off her desperation for soft and tender care and switched on the antidote – disgust for all her emotional needs.

Tucked in bed that night, she cried herself to sleep as she tried to please her body to make up for the absent embrace from her parents when they'd reunited at the petting zoo. Once again, the realization that she couldn't count on them for solace and love made her curl up in a ball and disappear under the covers. A new set of layers had been woven onto her cocoon to make sure that these dangerous feelings – this desperate need for care and attention – would never come out and disgust her again.

The next two years went by in much the same way, as Christy entered third grade. She kept herself almost invisible at home so she didn't have to feel like a burden to her mother. She blossomed when her father sat with her and helped her with her homework, and thrived on those rare occasions when her mother took her and Sarah to the park to feed the ducks stale bread. When her family rescued Bruno, a German Sheppard puppy, his unconditional love saved her from dying inside her ever-shrinking cocoon. Now she had someone to love, hug, talk to and play with. Bruno loved to be stroked, and he repaid her by snuggling up near her when she did her homework. He never tired of her insatiable need for his licks, his pawing and the feel of his fur against her skin.

It was hard not to burst with pleasure when her father took her for her first bike ride when she was nine years old, or when she'd just turned twelve and he camped out with her in the yard one summer weekend, listening for the crickets and boiling water over a portable stove to make hot chocolate before bedtime. Christy tried to etch those magic moments into her memory so that she would always have proof of her father's love and caring.

But the experiences were tarnished as soon as they got back inside the house when her mother called these escapades "unnecessary indulgences." Her father put up no defense, trying instead to appease his wife, who rattled off dozens of ways in which Christy had to pay for the stolen moments of closeness she had enjoyed with her dad. There were extra chores and early bedtimes for a week, and if she didn't perform the tasks to her mother's liking, she would be admonished. The worst part of it was that her father would join his wife in berating Christy about her lack of diligence. At every turn, what he gave he took away.

And yet, he would come to her when he was lonely and sad, pushed away by his wife's many physical ailments. It made Christy feel needed and valuable when he let her comfort him, but it was mixed with an iciness growing inside her. If being her father's sanctuary was the only way she could have a relationship with him, then she was willing to freeze her yearnings to be his adored "little princess." Of course, that meant she had to switch herself off and become a robot to keep the peace with her mother; then, if she was lucky, her father would seek her out for a little while and make her feel rewarded in the process.

For all her mother's moodiness, Christy loved it when they stopped to eat at the food court during shopping trips to the mall, especially when she was transitioning from elementary to middle school. Her mother actually asked her if she liked the food and promised that they would cook together at home. Sometimes she even told friends that her daughter was pretty, and occasionally she would buy Christy beautiful clothes, dressing her up with pride.

Overcome with gratitude, Christy would double her efforts to please her mother after one of these warm experiences. She'd do everything she could to prove she was worth it, hoping her mother would remember the promise to cook together. But invariably, the crack in the connection would occur as soon as they were back in the routine of family life, and it felt to Christy as if she'd dreamed those compliments, those warm eyes and caring words. She would almost kill herself to get that sense of togetherness back again, and feel utterly miserable when it failed. At first she was angry at this tantalizing mother who would come out and engage for a short time, and then disappear for eons. Then she turned the anger into a brutal force inside her, smothering her need to feel loved and lovable. Controlling her needs became a badge of honor, adorning her cocoon with strength and self-sufficiency.

In the middle of her thirteenth year, Christy started her period. One part of her was excited to be a woman and join the clique of girls who had passed through the door of womanhood and were now chased by boys. But another part was scared and upset. What if she had cramps, took time off from school, or needed money for sanitary pads? Would her mother hate her for heaping more problems on her plate? Would her father treat her differently? Would she have to relinquish Bruno, now that she was entering the adult world?

CHAPTER 7
RICK

"My love is as a fever, longing still
For that which longer nurseth the disease;
Feeding on that which doth preserve the ill,
The uncertain sickly appetite to please."

– Shakespeare's Sonnets, CXLVII

Alone and anxious about his parents' whereabouts the night they went out on the town in a desperate attempt to save their marriage, eleven-year-old Rick stayed up till the early hours of the morning waiting for a sign that would tell him if they were alive or dead.

By the time he heard his father's car pull into the driveway at 5:00 a.m., Rick's fear and anger had mixed into a volatile cocktail. He was speechless as his parents came through the door fighting, oblivious to the time and that he had been up all night waiting for them. He heard threats from one to the other as they raised their voices, each trying to outdo the other for the title of "Most-Wronged Spouse." He watched in horror as his mother slapped his father's face and his father grabbed her arm, twisting it until she cried out in pain. Outraged, Rick yelled, "Stop! You'll scare Beth!" But they ignored him as if they were unruly teenagers and he was the parent attempting to rein them in.

For the next month, Rick withdrew emotionally from his parents. He longed for them to come to him and apologize, but they were completely absorbed in their own drama. He tried to show them the agony he was suffering by being forced to take on the parental role in the family, but they turned a blind eye, trapping him in an impossible situation.

No matter how much he wanted to separate himself from his parents' failing attempts to reconcile, Rick was keenly aware that his mother was slipping back into a sad, dejected and hopeless place. He longed to know how she felt about her husband not being there for her when she was worn out or unwell. He wanted to unmask Angela so that they could deal with the reality of the situation together, but she refused to talk about her sadness or fears. He tried to be her savior and confidant, but she would get upset that he was neglecting his studies, causing her even more worry.

Rick often wondered what had gone wrong between his parents. What had made his father so disenchanted with his wife and family that he needed a secret lover? He remembered the fun times before Beth was born, when they went on picnics and paddled in the nearby streams and ponds. His parents had laughed and played with him, tickling him until he couldn't stand it anymore.

He loved going with his father to look at houses when he was on the job as a realtor, and getting a burger on

Rick

the way back. When they arrived home, he'd notice how much his mother adored his dad, delighting in his compliments on her looks and cooking. After dinner, his parents would often cuddle on the couch, allowing him to jump between them so that he could be included in the affection. Sometimes he crept into their bed and felt both their arms around him. Other times, they made him go back to his own bed, and he didn't understand why. At those times, he felt excluded and longed to be part of their special union again.

Riding with his father on the way to and from school was the highlight of his day. He loved their time together, conspiring to play tricks on Mom and tossing a ball around in the yard if he'd eaten his veggies. Rick could hardly contain his excitement when his father play-wrestled with him while his mother pretended to break them up, and they all ended up in a tangled heap, hugging and laughing. Life in those days had been so carefree, so full of joy.

But when Angela became pregnant with Beth, things suddenly changed. He remembered the day when he heard the shocking news that he was going to have a new brother or sister. It was what he had always wanted, but now that he was enjoying being the only child, it didn't feel so appealing. Now there was less time with his father, and his mother was often ill. From little Rick's perspective, he'd lost the magic he'd had with his parents, especially when they talked more about buying baby stuff than anything else. His whole world was rapidly changing, as his parents shifted their attention to the birth of their baby daughter, who entered the world when Rick was five years and three months old.

He didn't enjoy his fifth birthday as much as he had previous ones. He knew it was the last one he'd have alone with his parents, and his mother was already tired and distant. His father quickly gave him his present and then left for work. The party was just like all the others – balloons, party favors, cake, candles, fun games and a funny clown – but there was something missing. He already felt the intrusion of his sister and her stealing his precious relationship with his parents.

Rick couldn't penetrate the rapture that seemed to hang around mother and baby when they got home from the hospital, so he sought comfort from his father. But his father was impatient, telling him to "be a man" and help his mother by putting his laundry in the basket and remembering to brush his teeth after breakfast. He had to be quiet so as not to wake the baby, and worst of all, the baby got to sleep in his parents' bedroom. Rick knew he was no longer welcome when, one morning, as he tried to nestle between his parents and enjoy their embrace, he was told to "be more considerate."

He was miserable at school, constantly imagining that he was forgotten by his mother and father, now that they had a new baby. Maybe they loved a girl more than a boy. Perhaps they thought she was "good" and he was "bad" because he was greedy and wanted more of them. He tried his hardest to be quiet, thoughtful and kind, hoping to win his place back in his mother's affection and his father's good book.

Rick

By the time Beth was a three-year-old toddler and Rick was seven, life had become drastically different. Beth was "Daddy's little princess," always sitting on his lap, exchanging kisses and hugs, while Rick was shamed for wanting to do likewise. He felt left out, and if he whined or showed distress, his parents would tell him that he was the big brother and should "act like a man."

As his dad, Jerry, became ever more engrossed with Beth, Rick felt drawn to bond more closely with his mother. There was a tacit, mutual loneliness that brought them together, easing some of Rick's pain and fear of being usurped by his sister.

When Beth was old enough to go to school, Rick was already aware of his father's secret conversations with some strange person on the phone, whispering cooing words when his mother was busy with the dishes after dinner. He knew he had to save his family – especially his mother – from what seemed like bad things about to happen. But he didn't know what, when or how to do it.

Still in elementary school, he begged his parents for outings and activities on the weekend so the family could be together, but his father's boredom and his mother's despondency made his pleas fall on deaf ears. When he was halfway through middle school, the arguments between his parents reached a crescendo. As matters got worse, Rick took on more responsibilities, including babysitting Beth, to try and help his mother. His father was growing increasingly distant and his mother more depressed, as Rick started high school under a cloud of fear for his family's future.

CHAPTER 8
FEAR OF INTIMACY – SIGN 2: COMPLAINING ABOUT BEING BUSY

"It's only when we no longer compulsively need someone that we can have a real relationship with them."

– Anthony Storr

Nostalgia for the Christmas spirit back home in Britain enveloped me in December, and I gave in to the urge to make Christmas pudding laced with brandy. I scoured the specialty shops for marzipan and made chocolate truffles for friends and neighbors. I invited my British friends for a traditional Christmas meal and enjoyed watching DVDs of *The Forsythe Saga*, *Faulty Towers* and *Upstairs-Downstairs*.

Rick had taken me up on my offer of having phone contact during the break if he was having a rough time. In fact, he called me three times between Christmas and New Year, needing reassurance and approval about the way he was dealing with marital tensions, especially when his in-laws were visiting.

He resumed his sessions after the holidays, relieved to be back on a regular schedule, but on a cold but sunny Monday morning late in February, he was unusually late for his appointment. Ten minutes into the session time, I checked the waiting room and found him sitting there, curled up in a big beige sweater, unaware that he hadn't put on the call light to let me know he had arrived.

As he sat down in my office, he looked shriveled, as if the juice had been sucked out of him. Glancing at the clock on the side table, he remarked, "I didn't realize I was late… It's a bit embarrassing." He shrugged.

"Maybe you got here on time but didn't want me to know."

He shrugged again and pulled at a frayed thread on the cuff of his sweater.

"Did you want to come today?" I asked

"Yes and no!" he said, flashing a smile.

"What do you make of your ambivalence?"

"I feel shitty! I think I did something wrong with Christy, and I'm guilty and ashamed. I thought you would think badly of me."

"Maybe you wanted me to come find you in the waiting room so that you'd know I cared and you could feel better about yourself," I conjectured.

"I did wonder whether you would be glad to see me or not."

"Why is that?"

Sign 2: Complaining About Being Busy

"I was mean and ungrateful to you last time we talked so I wasn't sure if you would be okay with me today or not," he said.

"Sounds like you feel you have to be polite and compliant at all times," I commented.

"Well, if I were you, I would feel hurt and attacked for trying to be helpful, and I wouldn't want to put myself out again."

"So you imagined that I would only see the annoying parts of you and forget your nicer qualities," I noted.

"That's exactly how I felt when Christy blew *me* off!" he said, buoying up.

"Tell me more," I said, settling into my chair.

"When I'm affectionate and playful, it's as if she only sees bad stuff, like I'm being thoughtless and irresponsible."

"That must be hard on you."

"I feel so guilty and embarrassed."

"Just like you felt coming in today."

He nodded and started playing with the frayed thread again.

"Why don't you tell me what happened at home that's brought this to a head?" I prompted.

Rick cracked his knuckles and told me about the stressful morning three days ago that had tortured him ever since…

Christy was up at 6:00 a.m., packing her online sweater orders for shipping. Rick asked her to come back to bed for a cuddle, but she refused, saying she didn't have time to fool around.

A few minutes later, Joel ran in to play with him. At that point, Christy accused him of being irresponsible and acting like a child, with no concern for all the things that had to get done before they all left the house that morning.

Rick tried to fight against his hurt by remembering the joy he and Christy had shared the night before when they'd put Joel to bed and took turns reading him a story. Using this memory to give him courage, he offered to help with the school run, but Christy accused him of trying to placate her earlier fury when she accused him of playing with Joel instead of acting like a responsible parent.

******

Rick's voice grew raspy as he concluded the account of this demeaning experience.

"Maybe you imagine that I, too, will think you're a big baby and won't have any sympathy and compassion for you either," I told him.

"I do worry about that," he said, clearing his throat several times.

"I can see how confusing this is for you. When you're kind and nice, Christy tells you you're being childish and irresponsible. Yet when you own the fact that you may have been rude and ungracious, and expect to get punished, I treat you with care and understanding."

"Yup," he said, nodding.

"It sounds like you feel that everything is upside down and you don't know what to expect."

Sign 2: Complaining About Being Busy

"I help her with the housework and with Joel. I make life easier for her – so why does she act so cruel?" he asked, folding his arms against his chest.

"Maybe she imagines that if you offer to help it's a reflection of how badly she's doing the job."

Rick put a cushion over his abdomen, wrapped his hands tightly around it, and looked away. "Okay, I'm scared that you'll say it's my fault that Christy was short with me. But if she is stretched and stressed, why wouldn't she let me help her out in that moment, rather than seeing it as me judging her?"

"She let you get past her boundary walls when the two of you shared that joyful moment of putting Joel to bed, and then she threw you out. Maybe she knows that hurt you, and is anticipating your retaliation."

"But why doesn't she just apologize instead of being so harsh?"

"The happiness she felt when you put Joel to bed together set off warning bells inside her that she could become dependent on you."

"What's wrong with depending on me? I *want* her to need me!" he said.

"She probably has a whole list of 'what if' scenarios she's guarding against: What if you weren't there when she needed you? What if she wanted you and you weren't in the mood? What if she was hungry for connection and you were too busy?"

Rick dropped a cushion on the floor and picked it up.

"Something about what I'm telling you is uncomfortable. Does it remind you of something?" I asked.

"Yes," he said, meeting my eyes now, his voice cracking with anger and bitterness. "Like when I put all my trust in my dad to take care of my mom and he didn't!"

"I bet you never wanted to trust him again. I bet you just wanted to be so strong that you never *needed* to trust him again."

Rick nodded and looked sad.

"That's what Christy felt right after that contented parenting moment you'd shared the previous night. She didn't want the worry of wondering whether you would be as reliable again. So the next morning, she took action. She put all her focus on getting tasks done. Far better to let *you* be the one hoping, waiting and wondering if she would be available for you. That gives her the upper hand," I explained.

Rick's jaw dropped, speechless.

"You seem bewildered," I remarked.

"I am. I can't get my head around the fact that she wants me and needs me but can't trust me enough to rely on me, even though I've never given her any reason to doubt me."

"It doesn't make sense to you right now, but think back to the time when your father left you. What was it like for you to want a dad but *not* want him at the same time?" I asked.

"I was angry and just eliminated him from my thoughts," Rick said loudly.

"That's precisely the same dilemma Christy is faced with. She doesn't know whether to trust that you'll be available again, so she eliminates you from her thoughts

Sign 2: Complaining About Being Busy

by focusing on getting one task after another done," I pointed out.

"But I'm not a jerk like my dad!"

"Technically, you're right. But when she feels those confusing feelings of wanting you and not wanting you at the same time, it's as if you *are* her dad in those moments." I waited for him to absorb the comparison, then added: "You trigger those scary feelings, so you become the one she has to defend against."

"I feel like I have no chance when you show me how deeply rooted her issues are," he said shaking his head from side to side.

"What if you think about it in terms of chipping away at her fears so that you can offer her an alternative – one of safety and security?"

"I'm trying to do that, but it seems like an uphill battle I may never win."

"How about thinking of it as a journey to find stability and security, rather than a battle to win her over?"

"An endless journey seems so unpredictable."

"Right now, you're anxious about the future, and Christy also fears being lost. You cope by getting into battles, and she copes by having a constant routine of chores."

"But why does she complain so much about being busy and overloaded if she actually needs all those jobs to keep me far away? That seems totally crazy!" Rick said resentfully.

"How do you feel when she complains about her load?"

Rick thought for a moment and then replied, "I feel guilty and selfish at first. Then, when she refuses my help, I get angry and think she deserves to be stressed."

"Do you still feel like getting close to her when she makes you feel small and selfish?"

"No, I want to keep well away."

"When you buy into her portrayal of you as a selfish, irresponsible person and keep your distance, it's as if she has dodged the bullet and kept herself in her safe zone."

"But I offered to help out, so it's not fair that I get labeled as selfish!" Rick said, gesticulating wildly with his arms.

"When she feels attracted by your invitation to get close and have fun, she panics. But by turning you into the enemy, she can stop trusting you, thus saving herself from the catastrophe she anticipates."

Reassured that he wasn't to blame, Rick asked for a way to help him manage these swings in Christy's perception of him.

"Keep doing household tasks together, but expect that sometimes she will get scared and put her wall up. When she does, remember that it's your attractiveness that she's fighting against, so you don't have to feel guilty or selfish."

"I don't know if I can do that when she piles it on like that," he remarked.

"When Joel is having a tantrum and he kicks, bites and calls you names, you know it's temporary and that he'll be hugging you in a little while. It's similar with Christy."

That analogy rang true for Rick, and he looked at me to continue.

Sign 2: Complaining About Being Busy

"Think of it as a rope of connection between you. Joel lets go of it when he's having a tantrum, but you don't. If you show Christy that you're hanging onto your end of the rope, despite her efforts to chop it up, she'll come to appreciate your solidness," I explained.

"But what's the point of me holding on to my end of the rope if she doesn't even want to be connected?" Rick asked anxiously.

"It may feel like she keeps cutting off the rope or dropping it, but she is holding on to it – only more loosely than you are."

"How do you know that?" he asked, pulling his wedding ring off and then pushing it back onto his finger.

"Remember the moments you shared when you played with Joel and put him to bed together? You felt the closeness and connection because she was holding on to the rope."

Rick pursed his lips in disbelief.

"When she's feeling relatively safe, she will tighten the rope and pull you closer," I continued. "When she is scared and threatened, she'll loosen it and let you pick up the slack. But make no mistake, she has the rope firmly in her grasp," I reassured him.

"Hmm…" He frowned, pulling and twisting the frayed thread on his sweater.

"One of the ways you keep that rope taut between you is to tell her about your experience of feeling alone, taking care of your family after your father left. It will resonate with how she feels about taking care of her family now."

"But how is that going to get her to want to be close with me?"

"You're showing her that you've had the same experience as her, making her feel safer."

Rick nodded his head as if he were putting things together in a way that made sense. Despite his reluctance to relive his childhood, he conceded it might work, adding that he wished there was another way.

Two months later, Rick's frustration was back in full force. He felt that he'd taken two steps forward and five steps back. All the effort he'd put into doing jobs alongside Christy, sharing memories, and staying strong and available – no matter how many times she brought the axe down – was for nothing, he told me. If her intention was to completely destroy his love for her, then she got an A+. How on earth, he raged, was he going to counter her latest – and even more belittling – attempt to knock him off his game?

CHAPTER 9
CHRISTY

"We are healed by suffering only by experiencing it to the full."

– Marcel Proust

For three months, thirteen-year-old Christy managed to hide the fact that she had started to menstruate. She longed to talk to her mother about why she was bleeding from her private parts every month, and wanted to know how to handle the discomfort and shame when she was in school. But Sonia just gave her aspirin and told her to focus on her studies. Her father had been informed, but he avoided the subject entirely and became even less communicative. He no longer came to Christy for comfort and cheer, preferring to play with Sarah instead. Only Bruno's constant physical nearness helped ease the ever-increasing chasm that seemed to be growing between her father and her.

Her early teenage years were confusing, lonely and scary. Christy wished she could race to her sixteenth birthday, learn to drive and get away. It was hard for her to make friends and keep them because she was consumed with envy for their indulgent, luxurious lives. She survived by numbing herself when she was with them, hoping that some of their goodies would rub off on her. But alone at night, she would cry with frustration and outrage about the injustice of it all. Wasn't she as good, pretty and smart as those other girls? Why was she treated like a piece of furniture by her parents when all her classmates were fawned on?

Christy knew she couldn't compete with her younger sister or classmates for the attention they received, but she found she could get noticed by taking care of things for the adults around her. Volunteering to do small chores endeared her to her friends' parents. She was held up as an example of a "good girl," one who would make a good wife and mother. But as Christy aligned more with the older generation, it drove a wedge between her and her peer group.

As her sixteenth birthday approached, she fantasized about partying, drinking and picking up boys, but her mother had other plans. Her birthday party was nothing like those she had been invited to by her classmates. Sonia put her skills as an event planner into high gear and created a great party, but it was more for herself and her peers than for Christy. Her father hugged and kissed her, but was otherwise in the background. She hid her disappointment that her dad didn't show her off as his pride and joy by dutifully going through the games and activities her mother had organized, sad and dejected inside, acquiescent and grateful on the outside.

The following year, Christy got her learner's driving permit and began saving for a car from the money she got from babysitting and doing odd jobs for neighbors. She spent most of her time away from home, hanging with a variety of teen groups. She rebelled against everything her mother said, hoping her father would take her side, but he never came to her defense. He didn't even notice how beautiful she looked in her new clothes when her mother called her brazen and slutty.

Mark laid down the law about her going out with boys, because she could get into trouble and he wasn't going to tolerate that. But she defied him, because it was exciting when boys wanted to touch her. Once or twice, her father caught her being kissed and groped by a boy and he was livid, calling her all the disparaging names her mother had used to shame her. Christy was secretly elated that her father seemed to care so much, but at the same time she felt whipped for doing exactly what other girls her age did with impunity.

Besides, why was her father so mad? She didn't love these guys, and she wasn't being disloyal to her parents, so why was she "bad"? She wasn't giving the boys the part of herself that they wanted. All she was doing was getting the affection that her parents denied her. The making out was all over in a few minutes anyway, so what was the big deal? She couldn't live without these physically comforting and ecstatic experiences, so what was she to do?

CHAPTER 10
RICK

*"Being your slave, what should I do but tend
Upon the hours and times of your desire?
I have no precious time at all to spend
Nor services to do, till you require."*

– Shakespeare's Sonnets, LVII

At age thirteen, Rick felt caught between trying to be a good son and substitute partner for his innocent, suffering mother and getting on with his adolescence. The few friends that had moved with him to middle school were now in new groups, and he was left out. He hadn't felt comfortable hanging out with them when his mother needed him home, and now he didn't want to tell them that his father was a cheater who didn't seem to care about his family.

Rick's valiant attempts to support his mother and bring his father to heel consumed him until the day he heard his father yelling that he was leaving. Two weeks later, as Rick was approaching his fourteenth birthday, his father walked out with a suitcase and set up house with his girlfriend Wendy. This was no big surprise, but now it was real. Rick was now officially the man of the house, and the whole world knew about it. He often skipped school and hid the truancy notifications from his mother.

He lost interest in social studies, art and science, his three favorite subjects. As a young teenager trying to straddle the worlds of adulthood at home and adolescence at school, he felt alienated from his classmates and increasingly isolated. He hung out at the mall, smoking and drinking with older boys who let him into their clique in return for shoplifting food and sodas.

For a time, Rick felt hopeful that perhaps his parents were joining together to deal with his truancy, but it didn't last for more than a couple of months. His father gave him pep talks and promised to take him camping if he attended school regularly and got good grades in math and science, but these words were as meaningless as the love and commitment he'd once professed to his family. Rick would endure each "talking to" as a voice rang in his head, screaming at his father, *"You don't give a damn about me, so stop this charade!"*

He refused to go with Beth to visit Jerry and Wendy on the weekends. Part of him was angry with Beth for being disloyal, but another part liked the idea of having his mother all to himself. He felt wanted, needed and useful. It was as if he and his mom entered a bubble where they shut out the world and its ugliness, content to be a self-contained duo.

But when his mother went out with her brother and sister-in-law, or when she was invited to anniversary

Rick

celebrations and other events that excluded him, Rick felt cast aside. At those times, Angela would try and fail to persuade him to spend time with his father, as if forcing him to confront the reality of the situation. But Rick felt orphaned and retreated into an angry depression – until the next time they joined each other in the bubble. In the meantime, he endured the burdens and conflicts of playing protector, handyman and tenth grader who had to follow rules, take orders, and comply until he and his mother had their weekends alone again. Then he could just be his mother's companion and champion.

Each time Beth returned home after a weekend with her father, it was another intrusion into the bubble that Rick treasured. The tension in the house would rise as the clock struck 6:00 p.m. on Sunday nights, when Jerry dropped her off at the gate. Beth's excited talk about the fun she'd had with her father and Wendy made Rick bristle with rancor. He couldn't stomach the fact that his father was living some idyllic life while his "real" family was still suffering from his cheating and abandonment. Rick choked with bitterness and envy that Beth got to have good times with their dad while he lost out. Despite his loathing for his father, there was still a part of him that yearned for a loving connection, but he stifled it with great force when it popped up, determined not to be seduced into wanting that waster of a man.

Angela always welcomed her daughter back from her weekends away with an eagerness that made Rick nauseous. He felt discarded, traded in for a fresher companion who brought new things for the two of them to discuss and savor. He watched his mother planning things to do with Beth, as if she was competing with her estranged husband for their daughter's allegiance and love. Sometimes, he wanted to confront her and ask why she tossed him aside when he'd been so loyal, and demand that she acknowledge his unwavering care and support. Other times, he felt like a used tea bag, squeezed of all the flavor and color he brought to his mother's life, only to be trashed for another when he had served his purpose. Tortured by this conflict, he'd escape into a world where he imagined the loving family life he would make for himself when he was older, creating an ever more detailed montage of that life that cradled him in his worst moments.

CHAPTER 11
FEAR OF INTIMACY – SIGN 3: DOING GOOD DEEDS

"Everything comes to us that belongs to us if we create the capacity to receive it."

– Rabindranath Tagore

The weekend before our next session in early April, I had been unable to stop Rick's angry and dismissive tone from ringing in my ears. It seemed to be there when I woke up and followed me everywhere. No matter whether I was gardening, doing laundry or shopping, his protesting voice nagged at me. It made me feel that I wasn't any good at my job and that I was failing him.

I began talking back to his voice inside me, which brought some relief. I told him it seemed like all he wanted to do was complain about Christy and get my sympathy, without honoring his pledge to try to understand and include her experience in their dynamics. This calmed me, but on Saturday night I went to bed prepared for our Monday session to be the last. He was probably going to quit therapy and fire me. I wasn't able to relax on Sunday, so I set about getting things done around the house that had been put off for quite a while. By the time I'd prepared and cooked my dinners for the week, ate a meal and froze the rest, I got some respite from the anxiety about being axed the next morning.

Rick looked agitated when I opened the door to the waiting room Monday morning. He had a large bag full of camera equipment that almost knocked me over as he maneuvered it through the door of the waiting room into my office. He put the bag down and immediately started telling me how fed up he was with his wife and that he was considering leaving her.

As he settled into the couch, he said that he'd come home with Joel after father-son music class Sunday afternoon to find Christy busy vacuuming. She talked non-stop about the meal she'd prepared for them and insisted that he eat it right away. Then she accused him of not appreciating the fresh daffodils on the table, the trouble she took to make whole grain bread from scratch, and her attention to his preference for organic chicken and herbs. He responded by ignoring her need for recognition, angry that she hadn't even noticed that they had returned and didn't seem in the slightest bit interested in their experience of the class. He wasn't going to melt just because she was now anxious about his reactions. He silently gloated over the fact that the shoe was now on the other foot.

Christy reacted by taking out her anger on Joel, who was playing with his toys instead of eating. Joel's

Sign 3: Doing Good Deeds

distress sparked Rick into accusing his wife of being a mean mother.

That night, Rick reached the point where he didn't give a damn about Christy's fears. Her behavior was abusive, and he wasn't going to tolerate it any longer. At that moment, he vowed never to let her hurt him or his son again. He was going to stick up for himself by making *his* feelings and needs his priority, stomping over hers with alacrity.

Clutching his camera bag, he completed his justification for ignoring Christy's issues and then jumped into railing against me for expecting him to tolerate her abuse.

"What's it like being angry at me and Christy without censoring yourself?" I asked calmly.

"It feels good."

"What's the best part about it?"

"*My* feelings get to be important."

"They *are* important, but why do you have to wait until your rage reaches bursting point before you share them?" I inquired.

He put his hands in his lap and sat back silently, crossing one knee over the other.

"Seems like you dropped the rope of connection between you and Christy that we talked about," I observed.

Rick's shocked face told me that he had completely forgotten about the plan we'd discussed in our last session. I asked him to think back to the days prior to his latest tiff with Christy, and after a while he remembered sharing a childhood experience with her while doing chores together. "I told her about the time my parents went out and didn't come home all night," he recalled. "I shared how I had to be strong for my sister while I was freaking out inside. I told Christy how angry I'd been with them for making me worry so much."

"How did she respond?" I asked.

"Now that I think about it, her eyes lit up and she told me about the time when she was left behind at the fairground. She told me that she wanted to hug her parents and smash their faces in at the same time when they came back for her."

Suddenly, he sat upright in his chair and said, "I just realized that I feel exactly the same way now as she did then! When she lets me in for a tiny moment I want to hug her and never let go. But I also want to smack her for rejecting me for so long."

"So you made an emotional connection! She heard and felt your pain, and she also let you see and feel her pain. That sounds like a gigantic step forward," I noted.

"Yes, I guess so. But this last time, when she dissed me and yelled at Joel, was the limit," he said, the anger returning. "I can't live with these ups and downs. It's just too hard, and I'm not sure I'm up to it."

"I understand that you feel stretched to the limit, but look how quickly you forgot that magic moment."

Rick was quiet, and I sensed an opportunity to help him view Christy in a more sympathetic light.

"It's equally hard for Christy to hold onto those moments of trust and intimacy. Just as you get angry and fed up, she gets scared and feels unsafe," I pointed out.

He remained silent and looked very sad.

Sign 3: Doing Good Deeds

"I know you're still hurting from the last slap in the face," I continued, "but let's look at what was going on for Christy when you came home with Joel after the music class."

He tensed up and raised his eyebrows.

"She wanted you to notice the trouble she'd taken with the food and the flowers. She wanted you to attend to all her actions and love *those* things about her."

Rick was listening, taking it in as if he was watching a less-than-accurate remake of the same movie he had just shown me.

"She wanted her actions to be the focus of your praise, love and attention, so you'd be satisfied and not expect or ask her for any deeper emotional involvement."

Rick wriggled a little in his seat and put his hand on his camera bag.

"You look upset," I said.

"I feel like I messed up. If I had been more aware of what she was trying to do, instead of just being angry about her not letting me in, maybe things would have been better," he reflected.

"Perhaps. But some part of you knew she was avoiding you, and that was the part that got angry and didn't respond to her nagging for appreciation."

"It feels like whatever part of me I listen to, there's always another part that should be doing something else!" he said, irritated.

"Yes, you want her to welcome your love. But you also want to feel strong when she's rejecting you. She has the same conflict. She also wants to be close but strong, in case you abandon her."

He looked up, bewildered.

"That fearful voice inside her might be saying something like, 'If I do all these things for Rick and our family, then he'll be content. He won't need me to be emotionally available because I have filled him up with my unselfish deeds.'"

Rick grasped his bag handle. His chin was quivering as he tried not to cry.

"It feels awful, doesn't it, that Christy wants to palm you off with 'things,' when all you want is her company?"

He bent his head to the right and nodded.

"When you didn't make a big deal about the food and flowers, her anxiety level went through the roof. She must have been beside herself, thinking 'Oh, my God, if what I'm doing isn't making him happy, he might want me, the person – and I can't give him that!' She was in such a panic that she started to bombard you with questions to put the focus back on her good deeds."

Rick wriggled with discomfort, shifting around in his chair and staring into space. Then he looked at me with anguished eyes. "When you tell me what's going on in Christy's head, I feel like a pariah she's shielding herself against. It hurts so badly..." His voice broke as tears trickled down his cheeks.

"It's an awful feeling to carry around with you. Does it remind you of anything?"

Rick sighed and dabbed his face with Kleenex. As he threw the used tissue into the trash basket, he said, "I just had a flashback to the time when my mom used to come home tired from work, and I would give her a hug to try

Sign 3: Doing Good Deeds

and cheer her up. But she'd just tell me to get back to my homework and eat the meal she'd prepared."

"Sounds very similar to how you experienced Christy yesterday when you and Joel got home."

"Yes, I guess it does," Rick conceded. After a pause, he asked, "So am I feeling the same things now with Christy that I felt when I was a kid with my mother?"

"Yes. The same feelings get triggered, and it's very hard for you to tell the difference between what happened to you as a child and what happens to you now as a husband."

"How can I make myself stay with the husband part of me, rather than muddling it up with stuff about my mother?" he asked earnestly.

"It's putting your feelings into words when you reflect on a painful experience that begins the process of separating them out," I told him.

"In that case I'll be doing this forever!" he said disdainfully.

"When you can't see an end point, you don't know whether it's worth persevering or whether you should cut your losses," I pointed out.

Rick pulled his camera bag nearer to his body.

"It really throws me when she switches from being close for a short while to keeping me out for what seems like eons," he complained, pulling himself upright.

"You don't know what goes on inside her when she makes that switch and what sets it in motion."

"No, I have no idea. I don't see any signs, and I can't prepare myself. I have to be on guard all the time, which is tiring."

"Are you scared to know more about what goes on inside her, in case it's worse than you thought?" I asked.

"Yes, but I still want to know," he said, sinking down into the couch.

"When Christy makes great efforts to please you, she wants you to feel 'full' so that your emotions will be calm and quiet. You know, like when you have just eaten a really good meal and you are so totally content that you don't want or need anything else. Well, that's what Christy wants you to feel when she feeds you with all her good deeds."

Rick frowned as if I were talking mumbo jumbo.

"If you're 'satisfied,' then you won't need her to soothe any bad feelings. She's trying to make sure that you never get emotionally hungry and drag her into your web of bad feelings that might trap and paralyze her."

"So she just wants me when I'm up and not when I'm down!" Rick spat out in an angry, venomous tone.

"Not quite. She doesn't want to have to rescue you, because she's scared that if she steps into your world of bad feelings, all her stuff will get mixed in with yours and she won't be able to untangle herself or find her boundaries again," I clarified.

"It feels like I have to understand and make all these allowances for her, but she doesn't have to do the same for me!" he said bitterly.

"Isn't that the same feeling of injustice you felt when you made allowances for your mother, then felt scorched when she didn't reciprocate?"

Sign 3: Doing Good Deeds

Rick opened his eyes wide and stared at me for a few seconds before he slumped back into the couch. "It's pretty close. But why should I have to put up with it?"

"I know how frustrated you are, because you have been trying to right the wrongs done to you most of your life, and it's no different now."

"So what do you expect me to do?" Rick asked, exasperated.

At this point, I, too, was exasperated with his defeatist attitude, but continued on: "I know it's hard for you to see, but you aren't alone in this drama. Christy acts, and you react to it, and vice versa. You aren't in sync much of the time. That's why it's important for you to time your actions based on an understanding of where she's at. Then you won't feel so frustrated and burdened."

"Why doesn't she have to tune into *my* rhythms?" he complained. "Why do *I* always have to be the one trying to figure her out?"

"Because you are the one who's here, feeling rebuffed and wanting to get close."

Rick took a deep breath, as if he was fortifying himself against another set of onerous tasks I was going to lay on him. "Okay, what's the next step?" he asked half-heartedly.

Suddenly, I felt like keeping all my wisdom and advice from him. I realized I was as angry about Rick devaluing me as he was about Christy not appreciating him. With great effort, I held my feelings in check as I answered, "It feels dangerous to Christy when the boundary between you gets blurred. It's like being thrown into a sea of sharks that are going to eat her alive. She's fighting to keep herself distinct so that she can be a person in her own right, rather than just a 'thing' to be used for your comfort."

"If she hates having the same feelings as me and thinks I'm going to wipe her out, then how can I help her with her boundary problems?" he asked.

"Focus on her personal qualities, rather than her tasks and actions. For example, comment on how cute she is when she laughs at memories that the two of you share as you do the chores. Talk about her soft voice when she reads to Joel. Tell her how much you enjoy her humor, or her kindness when she lets you or Joel eat the last muffin at breakfast."

"I don't get how that helps with the boundary stuff," Rick said wearily.

"When you notice the softer, sweeter parts of her, then she, too, will pay attention to the nice, natural parts of her that are lovable. And if she feels good about herself, then she's going to feel more secure and less fearful that you want to rob her of herself," I explained.

"Yes, but what if she mocks me or attacks me for my comments?" Rick asked defensively.

Once again, I resented having to battle his innumerable "what ifs," but knew I had to persevere and be a good role model, so he could learn firsthand that it was possible to get past these scary mind-game obstacles.

"You may feel upset and want to withdraw or retaliate," I said. "But keep your eye firmly on the other side of her wall, where you know she has softness, love and a need for intimacy – even if she is isn't showing it at that moment."

I noticed the tiniest flicker of a smile on Rick's face. He had his hands clasped in front of him, but his body was open and facing me.

"Sounds easy to do, but I'm just not feeling confident it will work," he said dismissively.

I was overwhelmed with relief when the clock indicated our session time was over. His cynicism and self-defeating attitude lingered with me for the rest of the day. When I got home, I indulged in a glass of wine and some Belgian chocolates, contemplating why I wasn't getting myself a cat when I really wanted one.

CHAPTER 12
CHRISTY

"Nobody can hurt me without my permission."

– Mahatma Gandhi

Christy's newfound joy at being with boys was thrilling. They were always there, eager to engage in the touching, caressing and body-pleasing she craved. It was wonderful to have someone tune out the rest of the world and just enjoy her – much better than masturbating, and she didn't have to work at it or prove her lovability. The movement of their hands on her and their bodies around her, enveloping her in a tingling thrill, was more exciting than the affection she and Bruno shared. The heavy petting made her feel so alive – anger and disappointment just melted away. Pain and uncertainty didn't exist, and fear and worry simply turned to ashes when the fire of physical closeness electrified every cell in her body, bringing her to peaks of bliss that became her refuge.

She was finally in charge of her own happiness, able to access physical pleasure whenever she wanted to escape her pain and manage the anger that crept up when she wasn't looking. There were more than enough boys and men who wanted her, and she kept them interested by refusing to go all the way. She had plenty of orgasms without allowing them to penetrate her, and she wasn't about to let them invade her if she could get pleasure and relief without it. And she was always able to take the sting out of her mother's criticisms for not doing her chores by touching herself, alone at night in the sanctuary of her bedroom. Caressing herself in the most expert of ways took her beyond the pain of rejection when her father refused her help in the vegetable garden. And of course there was always Bruno, who never let her down when she longed for comforting emotional closeness.

One day, a few weeks before her seventeenth birthday, Christy's refusal to have sex with one of her regular heavy-petting partners backfired on her. Malcolm couldn't contain himself and he started to tear at her clothes. Christy bit him and scratched him until he gave up, leaving her stunned at how easily she had lost control. She couldn't possibly tell anyone about the incident (except whisper it to Bruno), but somehow, the story got out and spread like wildfire, even reaching her parents, who refused to forgive her or tolerate her shamelessness.

For the next two weeks, Christy's body reacted to the backlash with headaches, a urinary tract infection, and stomach bloating. She couldn't eat, and her condition became more serious by the day. She stayed in her room and allowed her mother to give her some medications while she made her plan of escape. She was going to run away and start a new life.

But her mother's concern about her infection made Christy put her plans on hold. It felt great to be fussed over, taken to the doctor, and let off household chores. Her father hovered at her bedside with special treats, offering to play their old, favorite games, and Sarah tried her best to make her big sister better. At last, Christy discovered what it was like to be the focus of attention, and the power of being sick. Now she was on a par with her mother, wallowing in the undivided attention of her family when she was under the weather. Her cocoon unfurled a little, letting in the long-awaited love that tasted every bit as good as she had imagined it to be.

Christy recovered with a mixture of sadness and excitement. Would her parents love her when she was not sick, or would they revert to treating her as a burdensome nuisance? In less than half a day, she discovered that getting better didn't feel as good as having all that genuine care and concern when she was suffering with a fever, unable to eat and in pain. If only she could get sick by wishing it, then she could have love and care on demand!

CHAPTER 13
RICK

"The great charm of your sex is its capability of an ardent self-sacrificing affection, and herein we see its fitness to round and complete the existence of our own."

– George Elliot, *Middlemarch*.

Things became tougher between Rick and his mother and sister when his parents' divorce came through six months before his seventeenth birthday. It was the final nail in the coffin of any hope he'd harbored to see his family restored. While one part of him was relieved that the ordeal was finally over, another part felt the pull of its permanence. Something important and vital had been broken. It was as if the divorce invalidated the union that had produced him. He grappled with the unsteadiness of feeling like he had no one to whom he belonged, and no one who wanted to claim him either.

Adrift in limbo-land, Rick now faced having to deal with the aftermath of the divorce on his mother and sister. Twelve-year-old Beth was now physically mature and, like any nubile preteen, wore revealing clothes. Rick found himself getting angry and upset about this. He came down hard on her for being "shameless" and encouraging boys to come after her. Part of him wanted to protect her, but a bigger part wanted to make sure she didn't become one of those women who tempted men away from their families. For a while, he and Beth were at loggerheads, as they acted out the roles of rebellious teen and prudish father. Rick felt as if he had to save his family all over again, trying to maintain a sense of decency and decorum while his parents indulged Beth's every whim, competing for her loyalty. Any attempt on his part to get his mother to take a stand on Beth's rebellious dress style, garish makeup and penchant for partying fell on deaf ears. It was almost as if Angela was getting some sort of vicarious pleasure out of allowing Beth to behave so brazenly.

But when Beth persuaded her mother to party *with* her, Rick nearly lost his mind. Everything that he held as right and wholesome, proper and worthy, was called into question. The more he tried to live by the rules, the more his mother and sister teamed up to break them, with no thought for the consequences. To Rick, it was as if they were abandoning him for an enticing world of debauchery, while he had to keep hearth and home alive as the sensible, reliable family guy.

He had already lost his father; then he'd lost his sister when she chose to maintain a relationship with their dad. Now he was losing his mother, too. Rick couldn't believe that after everything he'd done to take care of Angela and be her constant companion, she'd reject him and choose to act like the woman who'd stolen her husband away! How could she want to go out and flirt with other men? How could she desert him, knowing exactly what that felt like? What was so alluring about the world out there that he couldn't provide for her at home and during their weekends alone together? What was Beth giving her that he couldn't? And why was Angela choosing to change from a kind, selfless mother into a careless gadabout?

Rick was so infuriated with the way his mother and sister carried on that he often had the desire to throw in the towel, go out, get drunk and pick up girls. He knew that girls went for him by their seductive glances when he was at school or at the mall. Now that he'd passed his driving test and got a used car, there was nothing stopping him from being free to find some joy. He didn't owe anyone anything, and now that his mother and sister had broken away from him, there was nothing holding him back – except one thing: He didn't want to be like his father. He didn't want to fool around and shirk his responsibilities. He knew he had to graduate from high school and promised himself that up until that day he would toe the line and be a stalwart figure for his mother and sister. After that, he would make a new life – find a good woman, get married, have a family and never, never, *ever* cheat or get divorced.

CHAPTER 14
FEAR OF INTIMACY – SIGN 4: DISGUSTED BY CARING REMARKS

"The way you see people is the way you treat them, and the way you treat them is what they become."

– Johann Wolfgang von Goethe

Through late May and early June, I watched anxiously as Rick's euphoria led him to think that he had finally cracked the secret code and got into Christy's emotional lock-box. He was like a child thrilled at discovering the ability to make the world do his bidding, wanting me to witness and applaud his victory. But his preening pushed me away, making me feel like an untouched, nutritious smoothie blended perfectly for his needs.

But then, one Monday in early July, Rick came in looking small, bewildered and off-balance. He wore a stained tee-shirt, torn jeans and sandals, revealing long toe nails. Over the past few days, his blissful connection with Christy had suddenly crumbled, and he was dumbstruck with disbelief.

"I just don't get it," he said over and over again. "I was beginning to feel like I had finally won her over. In fact, I was going to come here today and tell you that I didn't need therapy anymore because everything was fine. And then, boom, I got walloped."

"You seem stunned. Tell me what happened."

"What's the point? It isn't going to change anything. Maybe it really is time to give up this therapy stuff!" he said curtly.

"Now I know how you feel when you invite Christy to share her bad feelings and she rejects your empathy," I said after a brief pause to drive the point home.

"What do you mean?" Rick asked, sitting bolt upright.

"I saw your emotional bruises and offered to soothe and comfort you, but you pushed me away as if I were offering you poison. I would imagine that's how *you* feel when Christy snubs you."

I watched as he spaced out and took a visual tour of my office, as if he was there for the first time. Then, haltingly, he told me what had led up to his wish to stop therapy before everything came crashing down…

Christy and Joel had been in a power struggle over getting dressed and Joel was winning. Rick felt pulled to help his wife, but when he suggested that reading Joel a story and making the funny faces he loved might coax him out of his stubbornness, she scathingly ordered him to take over, since he had "the magic touch." Rick felt as if a bottle of acid had been hurled in his face and screamed

Sign 4: Disgusted by Caring Remarks

back that she was ungrateful and he would never help her again. But the sound of Joel crying suddenly forced him to take charge. This time it was him giving the orders, as he told Christy how to get Joel ready, which she did silently but without gratitude. As he stormed off to work, Rick felt disappointed, hurt and bitter, making him hard and icy towards Christy for the next few days.

As he finished telling this story, Rick's voice dropped and he looked at me in a pitiful way.

"That's a brutal experience for you to bear, especially since you've been walking on air recently about how good things have been between you," I said.

"There is just so much I can take, and I have reached my limit," he said angrily, squeezing a handful of tee-shirt.

"I know that right now the rope between you and Christy feels sadistic," I acknowledged.

"I don't want that rope at all!"

"So now, you don't want the closeness. Is that how you felt when your mother derided your efforts to be helpful and make her happy?" I asked.

"Yes! I'd get really mad and not want to bother ever again. But why do we always have to go back to me and my mother?" he whined.

"Because the same part of you that wanted closeness then wants it now," I explained. "The same part of you that felt trashed then feels it now."

Rick twisted his watch strap several times.

"I want a romantic intimacy with my wife. That's not the same as what I wanted with my mother," he countered.

"But you haven't updated your methods."

"Wouldn't you react the same way if someone you loved kept shoving you away and then pulled you back for a little while before throwing you off again?" he asked defensively.

"It seems you want to pick a fight."

"Right now, I want to scream and fight, to force Christy to look at me with love. I want to yell at her for not treating me as important or special in her life," he growled.

"A moment ago, you didn't want any connection with her. But now, you're right back in there, inflamed with the desire to *force* her to value and love you," I pointed out.

Rick's lips curled into a faint smile.

"What are you smiling at?" I asked, curious.

"You see right through me. It's great, but it's also irritating."

"What's the irritating part?"

"I feel like Christy is the problem, but you keep pointing it back at me," he declared.

"Does fighting with me and trying to destroy our relationship make you feel better?"

"This is not a relationship, so how can I destroy it?" he asked sarcastically.

"If it's not a relationship, what is it to you?"

"I come here for help so I can get my wife to be more intimate; I don't come here to get to know *you* or anything," he said, thrusting his hands in his pockets and stretching his neck with an air of superiority.

"Whatever you come for, you receive it through our discussions, and our discussions are built on a relationship of trust and safety."

Sign 4: Disgusted by Caring Remarks

Rick frowned, and then his face crumpled. He fought back tears as he said, "I know you are there for me, but I want it to be Christy."

I flashed back to the times in my life when I'd wanted my parents to play with me or take me to school, but it was always the nanny and it was bitterly disappointing, even though I adored her.

"I understand why you feel so hopeless, but don't discount your successes. You've got past Christy's shield of chores, her complaints about being busy, and her wanting to palm you off with 'things,' rather than herself. You've also had moments of humor and softness, when you remember to hold onto that image of the connecting rope," I reminded him.

"I don't want to do any more work!" he burst out defiantly.

"Perhaps you're scared that if you keep putting all this effort into the relationship, the rewards will not be consistent and meaningful. That's exactly what Christy feels when there's closeness between you. She has been repeatedly burned and doesn't want to risk more hurt."

"What do you mean?" he said, bristling. "I'm not like her at all! I don't abuse her and reject her," he snarled.

"Just as Christy spurned you when you reminded her of her ability to coax Joel with stories, so you are spurning me when I remind you of your successes."

Rick grunted.

"If you can look inside and see what makes you do that, knowing that I have always been there for you and have never hurt or abused you, then you will understand why Christy rejects you," I suggested.

"I feel like a failure when I have to keep coming back to you with more problems," he admitted irritably.

"Christy probably feels like that too, only more so. To feel weak and in need of support is disgusting to her. Her tongue-lashing of your kind and understanding words makes certain you stop. She's saved from self-loathing and gets to feel strong and self-sufficient instead."

Rick had that faint smile on his face again.

"I hate it when you show me that I do the same things."

"Ironically, that's one of the things that keeps you apart. When you showed her how much easier it was for you to manage Joel than it was for her, you came across as superior, even though you were trying to be helpful and understanding."

"So I'm screwed either way! If I help, then I'm making myself out to be better than her, and if I don't help, then I'm a bad, insensitive husband!" Rick said angrily.

"I can see that you feel trapped," I said, "but there is a way out."

"Really? Tell me how," he dared.

"You want Christy to depend on you, to need you and love you because you make her feel good. The point is, she doesn't *want* to depend on you, because it makes her feel like she's a child again."

Rick winced, looking hurt.

"What's upsetting you?" I asked.

"I wanted to be the man my mother could rely on after my dad left us," he said, choking back tears. "The worst part of it was that she was happy to need and depend on

Sign 4: Disgusted by Caring Remarks

me sometimes, and then other times I might as well not have existed," he said, sobbing.

"And now you are going through the same heartache again," I said softly.

Rick took a few moments to collect himself, then gave me a look that told me he was ready to resume.

"When you felt so insignificant to your mother, what did you do to protect yourself from getting hurt again?" I asked.

"I thought that one day I wouldn't need any of them – not my mom, my dad or anyone. I would become a famous photographer and show them!"

"So you distracted yourself because you didn't want to feel the pain of being dependent on family to make you happy. That's the same thing Christy is doing now. She's protecting herself from being dependent on you by trying to do everything herself."

Rick shifted in his chair and started massaging his thigh.

"How are you feeling right now?" I asked, wondering if he was in pain.

"I'm getting anxious because so far it feels like we are as messed up as each other."

"Christy feels safer when she manages by herself. Reproaching herself with disgust when she senses her need for you is a good way of keeping those dangerous feelings at bay."

"But we've got to be different *somehow*!" he insisted.

"Your mother's neediness was attractive to you – it filled you up and made you feel important. But Christy experiences your wish for her to need you as a disguise. She thinks that if she responds, you'll whip off your mask of caretaker and become an insatiable leech, wanting her to take care of you instead – just like it was with her dad."

"There you go again. Christy and her dad!"

"Are you jealous that she had an emotional connection with her dad, even if it was bad?" I asked.

"That's ridiculous!" he scoffed.

"*Her* dad never left his family, and maybe that irks you."

Once again, Rick's eyes brimmed with tears, and his face turned red.

"It really hurts you, doesn't it," I remarked. "How did you feel when you ached for your dad on the nights he was out, or after he left you for Wendy?" I asked.

"I hated it and I squashed it."

"You were probably disgusted with that childish part of you that could have any need at all for your dad after what he did."

Rick shrugged his shoulders.

"That's how Christy feels when she has a need for you to show her how to do things. If she lets you support her, she'd be admitting her failure and neediness. But if she hears your words as accusatory, then she can use them to activate her self-disgust about needing help… Do you see that?" I asked, leaning forward.

"Then what am I supposed to do?" Rick exploded. "Never care? Never offer support? That's what I was going to do when I came to see you today. But I don't want my son to have two screwed-up parents," he said, growing agitated.

Sign 4: Disgusted by Caring Remarks

Rick's wish to give his son a better childhood than he'd had was a shining light in his otherwise dark portrayal of married life, and I commended him for it before suggesting the next set of strategies to cope with Christy's fears.

"When you feel Christy push you away with an insult or scornful remark, give her immediate feedback about your reaction," I urged. "You can say things like, 'It hurts when you push me away!' or 'I feel sad and rejected when you won't let me co-parent our son with you.' Or, try this one: 'It's disappointing when you turn my love into something evil. It makes me feel bad!'"

"But isn't that going to make her feel even more in control of me?" Rick wondered.

"Once you get her attention by messing with her game, she will show remorse, wanting to make up for hurting you. You will have made a direct hit against her defensive wall."

Rick looked skeptical, yet eager to find out more about how this plan might work.

"It gives you the chance to build a bridge of intimacy by saying things like, 'I want to learn how to make Joel laugh like you do,' and 'I'd like to show you how to get him to do as he's told when you're facing a time crunch,'" I said, offering concrete examples.

He sat still and listened before reverting to his familiar doubts about disclosing his reactions to his wife. He feared it would make him look weak and encourage her to take advantage of his vulnerability by being even more uncaring. Still, he left the office that day promising he would try my suggestions.

Now You Want Me, Now You Don't!

As I waited to find out whether Rick would choose to have a stable and fulfilling relationship, or whether he'd prefer to stay on the roller coaster, I took care of myself. I recharged my run-down batteries by making fresh salads with greens, peppers, strawberries and Tuscan melons from my garden, and a vinaigrette dressing made with three different basil varieties I'd grown myself. And there was nothing quite like fresh, crusty bread with tons of different cheeses to go with my salads! Even if Rick wasn't going to taste the emotional "smoothie" I'd offered him, I had to nourish myself with delicious, wholesome food, bracing for the next round of defenses he would put up against me.

CHAPTER 15
CHRISTY

"Let us learn to appreciate there will be times when the trees will be bare, and look forward to the time when we may pick the fruit."

– Anton Chekov

Defeated by the recovery from her urinary tract infection and the subsequent loss of attention, Christy became angry and depressed. She had been careless about her cocoon when she was sick. Allowing herself to be seduced by the love she got made her feel like an addict wanting another fix after a relapse. She thought of going back to the boys she'd enjoyed making out with, but she was scared that they would want more than she was willing to give. And besides, their fleeting physical affection had lost its appeal when her illness allowed her to taste the warmth and care of her parents.

Foiled by every attempt to regain her mother's concern and her father's affection, Christy began to hatch a master plan. Over the next year, she rehearsed leaving her parents' home and repeatedly imagined their alarm and regret at not having taken better care of her. In those moments, her vindictiveness gave her a superhuman strength that coiled her up inside her cocoon, tighter and tighter, until there was not even one air pocket left for her neediness to breathe.

She survived her seventeenth year by feeding on the revenge she was planning to take six months after she came of age. She was determined to make her parents honor that milestone day with an elaborate party – and they did. But Christy was there in body only. She felt good that her parents were "doing their job" by planning a celebration, and she made sure they didn't get let off the hook for a second for what she deemed both their duty and her entitlement. She encouraged them to sacrifice and spend money, taking secret delight in their worry about finances. She did everything she could to shame them into doing for her what her classmates' parents were doing for them, especially since they weren't buying her a car or even contributing toward one. She felt they deserved to be unsettled and suffer on her account.

Hardened to her mother's moods and her father's exhaustion, Christy talked about going to college. She wanted to study dance and drama, but her parents couldn't have cared less about her desire. Instead, her mother talked mainly about Christy doing more household chores and taking a bigger role in bringing up Sarah, while her father lectured about being "practical" and earning a living by doing "real work." Neither of them ever mentioned that she might fall in love, get married and have a family. It was as if they didn't think she was lovable or normal enough to go down that traditional road. This total disregard for her femininity and sexuality pierced her cocoon with flames of burning rage, but rather than perish in the fire, she used her fury as fuel to bolster her energy for the punishment she was about to dish out. The only time she gave herself a break was when her dog Bruno came to her room at night for his cuddle. At those times, she softened, allowing him to nuzzle her as she sensed their impending separation. Then she would masturbate to forget the pain of leaving him before falling asleep.

For two months after her eighteenth birthday, Christy acted as if she was going to college. She filled out forms, looked at course details, and talked out loud about her impending adventure. Her parents made no offer of financial, moral or emotional support, preferring to focus on Sarah's habitual temper tantrums about going to school, which sucked the attention away from Christy's plan. She upped the ante by announcing her departure date, but no one reacted. She bought an old car on its last legs to prove her intention to leave was serious, but her parents seemed oblivious to this "threat" and stayed focused on Sarah's behavior – clearly their main priority. They even tried to enlist Christy in sorting Sarah out, but she had already resolved to let go of any guilt or responsibility towards her family. She was desperate to shift the focus back to herself in a last-ditch attempt to get some sign of love and caring from her parents.

A week before she left, her car broke down. It was beyond repair, and there was no way she could buy a new one. Upset at knowing that her parents were not going to acknowledge her departure, Christy quietly packed her things and slipped out of the house after midnight without a word to anyone. But even though she had carefully sealed herself up in her cocoon, the fact that they took no notice was a crushing blow that made her dizzy and nauseous. Using money gifted to her on her birthday, she left on a Greyhound bus, traveling 900 miles to Taos, New Mexico, still hoping that her parents would come after her and want to make reparations.

CHAPTER 16
RICK

"The remote worship of a woman throned out of their reach plays a great part in men's lives, but in most cases the worshipper longs for some queenly recognition, some approving sign by which the soul's sovereign may cheer him without descending from her high place."

– George Elliot, *Middlemarch.*

A year after his parents' divorce, Rick continued acting as the man of the house, but he stopped trying to forge that special liaison he'd had with his mother. Instead, he had one night stands with women he met at bars and strip clubs that his old, truanting gang friends slipped him into.

During the day, he put energy into building his future when he graduated with his high school diploma. He dreamed about being a famous photographer with his work on huge city billboards, going viral online, and on hot, trendy merchandise. He imagined his father eager to claim him as a son again when he had name recognition. He envisioned his mother and sister feeling proud and trying to ally themselves with him. He fantasized about spurning them and finding a woman who would be everything that his family was not.

The year before he graduated from high school, Rick righteously performed his manly duties around the house but removed the job of "Companion to Mother" from his list. The power to control his life and satisfy his sexual needs without feeling like a cheat gave him strength to withstand the overtures his mother made when Beth, friends, or relatives were not available. Except for that time when Rick's father announced he had set a date to marry Wendy in two months.

His mother fell apart at the news and Rick's heart broke for her. She had handled the divorce by going out partying with Beth, but she cried a lot, lost her appetite, and had trouble sleeping. As Beth joined her father in the wedding plans, Angela turned to Rick for solace, and he spent his weekends back in the bubble with her for five weeks before the wedding. She was warm, loving and eternally grateful to him for being such a steadfast, loyal and reliable son, even singing his praises to her side of the family. As a result, his aunts, uncles and cousins all spoke highly of him, and he was uplifted to a place of honor in the family, making him feel justified for breaking off contact with his father.

Rick anticipated each weekend spent with his mother before the wedding with a mixture of joy and dread. He felt vindicated, now that she had revived their close connection. It was as if some sort of justice had been done, so he allowed himself to feel wanted, special and important to her. Now he was able to detoxify the poison that his father had fed her and restore her vibrancy. He slipped into that old familiar, comfortable rhythm of their togetherness, feeling it was all that mattered. They enjoyed DVDs, game shows and reality TV. They also talked about how things would be after Rick graduated from high school. At those times, he was torn between wanting to reassure his mother that he would never leave her and holding onto his plans to make a new life for himself away from the family.

Then suddenly, two weeks before Jerry's wedding, his mother became irritated. She no longer talked about what they would do together on Friday night. Instead, she went out with her relatives and friends, leaving no time for the two of them to be with each other as the dreaded day approached. Rick was stunned, and deeply wounded. He hadn't cried in a long time, but he couldn't stop the tears from cascading down his face as he sat alone, ditched and discarded again by the very person he had rescued and rejuvenated. The pain burned his insides raw, and this time he didn't hesitate to drink the remainder of the bottle of whiskey his father had left before he walked out. The alcohol tasted awful, but he had to get back his strength and resolve, and this seemed the only way he could do it without crumbling into tiny pieces and ending his life.

Once again, Rick had been thrown out of a mutually loving embrace and into the wilderness. He revisited his plans for life after high school and was determined not to let anything or anyone lure him away. He wasn't going to wait around till the next time his mother needed him when she had a meltdown or looked to him to discipline Beth. He was going to get that diploma, toss his mortar-board cap in the air – and take off!

CHAPTER 17
FEAR OF INTIMACY – SIGN 5: MISTRUSTING CARING ACTIONS

*"Realize that your inner sight is blind
and try to see a treasure in everyone."*

– Rumi

For the next three months, it seemed like Rick and I were playing a cat-and-mouse game. He'd tell me that our sessions were really making a difference in his marriage and that he wanted to go at a quicker pace. But when I gave him more advice and encouragement, he dove into his mouse hole and hid, saying that he had exaggerated how good things really were. At that point, I felt powerless, forced to retreat into my own mouse hole until he re-emerged before resuming the conversation. Often he'd rave about a self-help book or DVD that he claimed was so much more helpful than our sessions, ramming me into my mouse hole again. Then he'd lure me out with flattery, which I knew was a sign of his desperate need to feel my caring. Reeled in, I'd soften – only to get scorned and compared unfavorably to some Dr. Phil character he'd watched on TV.

I found myself nodding off in session when he went on one of his long rants, devaluing my efforts. The clock became a source of comfort as I kept watching, longing for the session to end. My mind wandered to the dinner I would enjoy later that night, or how I would write about working with difficult clients on my website blog.

The days between his sessions were such a relief! I couldn't wait to get home and de-head spent flower blossoms, hoe the weeds in my vegetable beds, and cut some rose-scented geranium sprigs for my bed and bathroom. Thoughts of becoming ill or having some emergency arise Sunday evening became the norm, and I fought them with as much professionalism as I could. Even the most hateful job of raking leaves became a joyful release from the cage I felt locked in when Rick showed up for his regular Monday appointment to beat me black and blue.

During a session a couple of months before Christmas, Rick mentioned that he was sharing his feelings with Christy about being pushed away and using the image I'd suggested of a rope between them to hang onto their connection, despite her negative reactions.

"How did that work for you?" I asked.

"Better than I thought it would," he responded. "A couple of times, I saw her stop herself just before she scolded me. Her face changed, and her voice wasn't so harsh."

"Do you feel any closer to her now?" I inquired.

Sign 5: Mistrusting Caring Actions

"When she lets me in, I get excited and want more. But then, at the eleventh hour, she backs out. It's absolutely maddening, and at those moments, I just want to shut her out!" he said, his cheeks reddening.

"Does that feel familiar?"

"It's what happened with my mother. I would ignore her when she wanted my company after she ditched me for her other relatives."

"So you cut off the relationship in order to take revenge," I pointed out.

Furious at me for holding up this mirror, he stormed out of the session ten minutes early.

Part of me expected Rick would quit therapy because I had upset him. But another part sensed that we had a strong enough bond to allow him to come back the following Monday and work out his anger and disappointment with me.

I was right.

Rick did show up for his session, seven minutes late, a bit sweaty, in a jogging suit and sneakers. He strode into the office, plopped onto the couch, splayed his knees, and immediately bombarded me with his latest tale of rejection by his cruel wife. He spoke quickly, oblivious as to whether I was tuned in. I settled back in my chair, relieved that he had shown up, but concerned that he was bypassing the issue of how the previous session had ended. Instead, he proceeded to tell me how Christy was accusing him of wanting to spend time with his family, who were vacationing in the area, and leaving her out. In the past, he'd begged her to accompany him when family or friends came to visit, but she always declined. She had an open invitation, he said, to join him whenever she wished, and he was incensed that now she was denying he'd *ever* invited her to come along.

******

When he'd come back from his visit, Christy was already asleep, but just as he turned the light out on his nightstand, he felt her stirring. She woke up and, without a word, grabbed onto him and started to kiss and fondle him. He was still upset about her unjust accusations and wasn't in the mood for sex. But something about the way she touched him made him soften. It was as if she wanted to be close but just couldn't say it. His instinct was to turn around and snub her just when her need for him was most apparent, but he found himself aroused, and after a minute or so of her caressing him, he made love to her. She couldn't get enough of him, holding him tight as if he were about to disappear and be lost to her forever. He felt as if she wanted to devour him whole. He got excited by her voracious appetite but felt uncomfortable by the aggressive way she was pulling at him, moving him around to satisfy her physical needs. She sat on top of him when she wanted control, and he felt like he had to surrender to her urgency and rhythm. His climax was physically relieving but emotionally unsatisfying.

Rick didn't sleep much that night. He was plagued with the question of why Christy would want to "gobble him up" so voraciously, when earlier that day she had accused him of excluding her from his family visit.

The next three days were full of tension and anxiety, as Rick juggled his need to get back on speaking terms with Christy and his determination to prove he wasn't selfish about seeing his family. Then, a miracle came along to lift him out of his morass. He received a call from his friend Paul, who was returning from a long trip abroad, and it sparked an idea. He would craft the perfect plan to show Christy how wrong she was – and he couldn't wait to implement it.

Christy was delighted with Rick's invitation to come with him to meet Paul. At first, he was a little disappointed that she responded so well, because it killed his effort to vindicate himself. But he sloughed off that initial setback, imagining how great it would be to enjoy the company of his wife and good friend at the same time.

Yet, when the day arrived for them to meet at Rick's favorite restaurant, Christy pulled out. She was wound up in a ball of anxiety. A whole host of worries took the place of her initial enthusiasm for the night out. What if Paul didn't like her? What if Joel got sick while both his parents were out?

******

As he finished telling me how Christy had pulled the rug from under his feet, Rick looked at me with a blank expression.

"How are you feeling now?" I asked.

"Angry! Just when I thought things were working out, everything fell apart. It's like when I thought I could get Dad to stay with us instead of going to Wendy; he would say yes in the moment and then make all sorts of excuses later."

"What would have made you feel better?"

"Telling him what a useless father he was!" Rick said in a loud, shaky voice.

"But when you couldn't do that, you felt empty."

He nodded.

"You spent the first fifteen minutes of the session playing the same cat-and-mouse games with me as your father played with you. But even though you voiced your anger this time, you felt just as empty," I said.

"I don't know how I felt," he said defensively. "It's *your* job to know that!"

I rewound the session and showed him that while he'd been spewing his bile I was prevented from comforting him, leaving him without any nutritious juices to take its place. He listened, shaking his head in denial, huffing and puffing, barely able to contain himself.

"How does all this apply to me and Christy?" he asked, fleeing.

"Okay," I said, annoyed by his evasion. "Let's focus on you and Christy. She took the initiative by telling you about her wish to be with you and your family. What do you make of that?"

"What are you talking about? She accused me of *deserting* her for my family," he said incredulously.

"The point is that she wanted to be with *you*."

"It drives me crazy. She says she wants me, then she refuses to come out with me, and then she wants to eat my body as if she were starving. What am *I* supposed to do?"

"That's a good question," I said. "If you remember Christy's frustration about her father preferring his wife to his daughter, then you might understand why she insists that you would prefer your family to her."

"So I have to keep proving that I'm not like her dad?" he said, flapping his knees furiously.

I bit my tongue, trying not to be as impatient with him as he was with himself.

"What was it like living with your girlfriend Dawn?" I asked.

"It was okay. What's that got to do with it?"

"Was it really okay? I remember that you were irritated with her for being so 'perfect.'"

"What of it?"

"You're bored by stable and predictable women. You want the power of molding Christy into your ideal of perfection. That's where the juice is for you."

"That sounds crazy!"

"Perhaps, but think back to how powerless you felt when you failed to make your parents stop fighting or to get your father to stop having affairs. It's unfinished business, and you are not done with it."

"Now I feel doomed."

"I think you have a deep wish to overcome your past and do it differently," I suggested.

"But how does that explain Christy's aggressiveness in bed after a row?"

"I wonder why you suddenly changed the subject," I said, taken aback.

At that point, Rick blew up and accused me of wanting to talk only about myself, instead of helping with his marriage. Then his indignation gave way to a lost and empty look, and I decided to help orient him by answering his question.

"That day, Christy wanted to visit your family as your 'special person.' But she was overcome with fear that you would prefer your family to her. So, when you got home, she wanted to physically 'stuff' herself with you in case there was none left for her when you got back. She thought you had given them your loyalty, and your body was the only tangible thing left for her."

"But why was she so aggressive?"

"She was angry at you for stirring up those feelings of being second best."

Rick buried his face in his hands and shook his head, stifling sobs as his chest and shoulders heaved with pain and sadness.

"You won't always be the perfect partner," I said, comforting him.

He perked up, tucking the hem of his shirt into his pants. Now he really wanted me to fill his emotional fuel tank with my care and empathy, so I continued: "If you allow yourself to be human, you will feel Christy's attempts to get closer to you," I said.

"How do I make sure I don't miss her next coming out party?" he asked sarcastically.

Sign 5: Mistrusting Caring Actions

"Let's check in and take your temperature before we go on."

He looked around the room, tapped his knee with his knuckles, and then said, "Better!"

"Okay. So when you let me in, you feel better and it helps revive your interest in the marriage," I observed. I suggested that we review how he was using the strategies I'd given him in our previous sessions. When he thought about each one, he realized that they had become routine and were operating reasonably well.

"You deserve credit for making it work," I said. You just get derailed when Christy throws you another curve ball, so let's add a new strategy to your repertoire. Any ideas on what you might do to continue chipping away at her wall?"

"I have no idea. Every time I try to think of ways to get through to her, I end up falling flat on my face," he admitted, retreating into his lost and helpless mode.

"I can see how scared you are of participating in this exercise. You want me to tell you what to do. Then you won't have to feel responsible if it doesn't work."

"I've already failed, so it's obvious that my way of thinking is useless," he said.

"The child in you failed because you were alone and desperately trying to fix an impossible problem. But now you are grown, and you have experience. You don't have to do it all yourself, and you are already notching up successes, even though they may seem minor to you."

Rick turned his head sideways and grinned with pleasure.

After a few seconds, I asked: "You mentioned that Christy seems to care about her impact on you. What if you told her more about your feelings in those moments?"

"What if she can't take it?"

"There might be times when she can and times when she can't," I said. "You'll have to gauge when she can handle it and when she is already too full up."

"But that's exactly the problem!" he exploded. "I can't read her, and I always end up getting it wrong."

"And yet, you know by now that it's not all black and white, either failure or success."

"I hate this in-between stuff. Why can't it be simpler?"

"It's confusing to you, but it reflects the depth and richness of your emotional life with Christy. For example, in the situation where she backed out of meeting with you and Paul, you could have said something like, 'I'm so disappointed that you won't be with me to share this reunion. It was really important to me.'"

Rick looked uncertain, so I added, "Sharing your feelings forges a connection. It gives Christy the message that you want to come out of battle mode, reconcile, and get close."

"I like the idea of sharing my disappointment, but I don't want to risk getting depressed if the only thing I will feel is sad," he said quietly, twirling his finger around a spot on his scalp.

"When Christy responds by tuning into your feelings, it cheers you up," I reminded him, "and you can refer to that anytime you fear getting overwhelmed with sadness."

Sign 5: Mistrusting Caring Actions

Rick left the session more grounded, with our relationship still intact.

A two-month stretch of calm washed over Rick as he got used to the fluctuations in the emotional climate of marriage. Then, one day in January, he suddenly accused me of being a fake! The so-called advice and "game plans" I'd given him were just shadows in the night, and their effectiveness was an illusion, he raged. Christy had just slapped him forcefully in the face because he'd complimented her on her ability to cope in a crisis. So how, he demanded, how was I going to excuse her cruelty this time?

CHAPTER 18
CHRISTY

"But that your trespass now becomes a fee;
mine ransom yours, and yours must ransom me."

– Shakespeare's Sonnets, CXX

Survival was Christy's forte, and she found a house in Taos to share with a couple of young women her age. The first month's rent used up most of what she had left of her money, so she grabbed at the chance to work in a beauty salon nearby.

At first it was great to feel independent and valued by the staff and customers, but by the end of her probationary month she was dejected and dragged herself into the salon most days. The hours were long, and she was literally cleaning up everyone else's mess. Neither of her parents contacted her when she sent them news of her whereabouts, and the long-nursed image of them groveling at her feet and begging her to return dissolved like fizz in an open can of soda. She didn't know what to do on her days off, now that her grand scheme had fallen flat. Most of the time, she felt sad and lost, longing for her father to come rescue her and promise that he would make up for all those missed opportunities of making her feel special, spoiled, number one and adored.

When her fantasies didn't materialize, Christy looked to life at the salon to pick up her spirits. But when the staff and customers treated her like a servant, family life looked rosy in comparison. She missed hugging Bruno and talking to her sister. She missed the familiarity of her mother's moods and her father's nonchalant way of relating to her. She hadn't believed it could affect her to this degree, but there was no denying it – she was homesick. There must have been some breach in her cocoon for this overwhelming despair to clutch at her insides and sap the energy and excitement of life that had flowed so freely only a few weeks ago.

Christy's only recourse against her homesickness was to distract herself with more things to do. For the first two weeks after her move, she took on the role of housekeeper for her roommates and basked in their appreciation. It kept her mind off the hope that her parents were pining for her. But as the novelty of her household chores wore off and the gratitude of her roommates dried up, Christy felt empty again.

Only one thing excited her – food: thinking about buying it, preparing it, cooking it, decorating it and making it into a work of art. It was as if she had created a custom-built curriculum just for her. She didn't need to go to college and study dance and drama any longer because she had it all at her fingertips. She went to the library and borrowed books on the cuisines of the world.

Christy

She watched all the cooking shows on television and became an aficionado of local produce. The subtle moves she made with ingredients choreographed brand new versions of classic recipes, as if she was dancing to a familiar tune, but one that had her unique take on it. She invited the salon staff for dinner parties and encouraged her roommates to bring guests to sample her culinary performances. Once again, the feeling of power surged through her waking moments, giving her energy and masking the hurt, pain and anger at her family for not showing sorrow and regret over her leaving.

Over the next year, Christy continued working in the salon while luring people to her home with gastronomic delights. But during those periods between her elaborate dinner parties she was left ravenous for company, admiration and adoration. At times, she could feel her defenses weakening and had to take urgent action to maintain her equilibrium. She deflected the panic of emptiness by stuffing herself with as much food as she could lay her hands on. The bloated feeling after binging was worth it. So was the discomfort of not being able to fit into her clothes. Anything was better than feeling rejected and disgusted with herself for wanting people to love her by savoring her food creations.

When her cooking failed to bring her the attention she craved, Christy put a new seal of varnish on her cocoon, determined to make it impermeable to the yearning for love and approval that crept up on her, no matter how forcibly she barricaded herself inside. But this time, she was determined to make a permanent seal to ensure she didn't get hurt again.

Eating large quantities of food at any hour, day or night, became her newest distraction from feeling sad, angry, disappointed and starved for love and affection. It worked like a charm. She put on weight and felt ugly. No one wanted her now. At last, she could stop working so conscientiously at trying to make someone desire her and choose to take care of her. What a relief! Closing the door on the possibility of being wanted and cared for was the only way she could keep the cocoon from disintegrating and failing to protect her.

She spent a lot of time in the library, hiding from the world while indulging her appetite for escape by reading travelogues and adventures of famous chefs trying out new and exotic foods. She dreamed of going on the same gastronomic journeys and started to look at the want ads for jobs that might take her far away so she could forget her parents, her womanhood, and the longing for a home and family of her own.

A few weeks before her twentieth birthday, Christy gave her notice at the salon and took a job as a nanny for two young children whose parents were going to Europe for a year as TV reporters for CNN. The couple were impressed with her housekeeping and cooking skills. They saw that she was good with the children and had no ties that would prevent her from giving full attention to their family.

Christy was both thrilled and apprehensive about her new job. She felt unattractive and burdened by her weight, but she knew that her asexual appearance was an asset, since it would not threaten her employers' marriage.

She didn't tell her parents about the job until she was in France, ensconced in her duties and ready to show them that she was thriving without them. But she went to bed many nights in a tearful state, trying to control the bouts of jealousy and anger that erupted when she saw her two young charges being adored and spoiled by their parents.

Comforting herself with romantic novels, food shows on television and masturbation worked for the most part, helping her get to sleep and manage the hectic schedule that each day brought.

Six months into the job, she got bolder and started to go out with other nannies she met through the children's school. On these outings, she came across many men who were only too willing to give her the physical affection and closeness she craved. Christy now wanted sex; she wanted to be desired and she wanted to be filled up. She wanted to give up her virginity and feel a like a sexual woman. She delighted in men's eagerness to get her clothes off and take her to heights of pleasure that far surpassed any of her ecstatic and relieving masturbatory moments.

She reveled in the excitement of meeting her lovers on her nights off, letting herself go in reckless abandon. Her weight and appearance were not obstacles – she was able to get men to want her and fill her up as many times as she pleased. She didn't have to pretend or hold herself back, and it was all deliciously sensuous, free of any obligation towards her lovers. They didn't want emotional ties, and she certainly didn't want to be responsible for their feelings or needs. It was just pure heaven, looking forward to new experiences, new sexual partners, and new levels of pleasure with no strings attached. Not wanting to risk pregnancy, she went on the pill.

During the second half of her year in Europe, Christy shed all the weight she had put on without even trying. Her sexual encounters fed her whole being in ways that nothing else had or could. It was invigorating to get her needs met without having to compete, get sick, or be a "good girl." The envy she had towards the children subsided, leaving her with just a hint of a wish that she too could find and enjoy a nice family life like they had.

Traveling with her employers to Spain, Italy, Austria and England for brief spells during that year abroad was a bonus. With all her expenses paid, she was able to buy herself nice clothes and flaunt her sexuality when she was off duty. It was nice to feel like someone's girlfriend for a few days, or sometimes even a few weeks, and then say goodbye without guilt when she moved on with her employers.

Often she felt like Jekyll and Hyde – the prim governess while she was at work and the daredevil femme fatale when she was off the clock. She could be the good girl during the day and the "naughty but nice" girl on her nights off. But how was she going to sustain this duality when her employers returned to the States in two months' time?

CHAPTER 19
RICK

"The fact is that love is of two kinds, one which commands, and one which obeys. The two are quite distinct, and the passion to which the one gives rise is not the passion of the other."

– Honoré de Balzac

For the next two weeks, Rick nursed his throbbing wounds from his mother's rejection with intricate planning for the future. The day he got his diploma, he was going to get his backpack, drive to Taos, and take pictures at the arts festival. He had already scouted some cheap places to stay while he looked for a job. All the years of being a handyman for his mother meant he could easily find work during the summer festival and tourist season. He was going to sell his pictures and start making a name for himself. He was also going to pick up girls and have a ball. The chains of responsibility were coming off.

His father's second wedding came and went without Rick's blessing or presence. He spent the day taking pictures on a nature hike near his home in Tucson, Arizona. He was determined to make a statement by doing something for himself, rather than for Jerry, and indulging in his hobby was the ideal solution. The silent, ageless stone along the mountain trail soothed his rage and deep sense of betrayal.

He spent the night under the stars in his tent, listening to music on his iPod until the battery went dead. But no matter how hard he tried to think of his upcoming graduation and all the parties lined up to celebrate, his mind kept shifting to his father. He had the same urge to smash Jerry's face in as he'd had when, at age ten, he'd first heard his dad talking to his lover Wendy on the phone when he thought Rick was asleep. He had wanted to unmask his father then, without his mother finding out, so he'd spent the next month glaring with accusation at Jerry whenever they were in the same room. He hoped his dad would get it and start acting like a proper husband and father again. But it didn't work. His parents thought he was just being moody because he hadn't settled in to middle school.

The sounds of coyotes and crickets lulled him into a restless sleep, and he woke in the early hours, cold, hungry, and relieved that the wedding was over. Although a great weight had been lifted off him, he wanted to rid himself even more completely of the past.

When he returned home, he found his mother arguing with Beth, who wanted to spend long periods of time with her friends and their families. It was almost as if his mother was trying to stop her daughter from deserting her, having failed to succeed with her husband. But this time, he didn't succumb to his mother's pleas for support

Rick

or her attempt to turn him into a substitute father for Beth. He took care of the household jobs that needed doing, but otherwise embarked on a separate life.

The four weeks prior to graduation were strained and uncomfortable. Rick distanced himself from his mother and sister's drama and hung out with his peers. He wanted to get a taste of being like the other guys, and he certainly wanted the admiring and lusty looks of the girls who were beginning to arouse his interest. He also wanted to show his mother what she had thrown away by spurning his love and devotion. He wanted her to realize her loss and beg him to be there for her again. He imagined telling her it was too late, that he was no longer available to be pushed and pulled according to her whims. The urge to make her hurt the way she had hurt him cloaked him in a thick, impenetrable skin that kept him hard and unrelenting as he executed his plan.

He drank himself silly and slept with as many women as were willing, often several in one night. He smoked weed, did cocaine, and took whatever pills were going around at the raves he attended. There, he could emulate the loathsome behavior he'd criticized in self-indulgent, irresponsible people, as if to nullify all the years he'd lived in a moral straightjacket. But after six days of nonstop abandonment, he felt sick and unsatisfied. He didn't enjoy the company of this rowdy, impulsive group. He found them immature and unsubstantial. Other than joining them in binging on booze, drugs and sex, they had nothing in common. He didn't belong with this crowd, but he didn't have anything else to be part of either.

Rick was, however, drawn to one of the girls in the crowd who also seemed uncomfortable with their recklessness. Dawn, a few months older than him, was a classmate at his high school, and had an air about her that made him feel like they were on similar turf. She was an only child who took care of her elderly, sick father while her young mother gallivanted with friends. The affinity that Rick felt with Dawn was wondrous and remarkable. It was almost as if he'd recreated the bubble he'd shared with his mother, but this time with someone who, like him, wanted a more intimate friendship.

For the first time in his life, Rick found an easy compatibility with someone outside his family. They melded together as they exchanged the pain of their respective childhoods and their longing for peace and stability. He wanted to spend every waking moment with Dawn, but he'd promised himself he'd be the "man of the house" up to the day he graduated from high school, and he wasn't going to renege on that now.

He saw Dawn as much as he could. The nearness of her melted away any guilt he felt about not being his mother's right hand anymore. As Rick felt more anchored in his burgeoning relationship with Dawn, his plans to go to Taos and start a new life faded. But he also had moments of panic when he woke up from a scary, recurring dream in which Dawn had tired of him and left. At these times, the idea of Taos seemed inviting, compared to committing to Dawn and wondering whether she'd turn out to be like his mother, wanting him one minute and pushing him away the next.

Rick

Graduating with Dawn by his side boosted Rick's hopes for his future. They pooled their money and rented a studio apartment, living as roommates, free at last from family duties. She worked in a frozen yogurt outlet, bringing home what was left over each day for the two of them to enjoy while watching their favorite programs online. Rick joined a handyman crew and was out on jobs at all hours, but he got good tips, and together they could afford the rent and utilities.

Rick lived in constant fear that Dawn might feel "second best" and leave him when he took time away from her to attend to his family. Likewise, each time she had to take care of emergencies with her father, he feared she wouldn't come back, that he hadn't done enough to make her want to return, or that she would feel he was just one more burden for her to shoulder. He worried that Dawn's guilt about leaving her father would make her choose her old life again. These obsessive thoughts were gut-wrenching. Living in a state of suspense, he constantly made plans to spoil Dawn, take better care of her, and prove to her how important she was to him. His fears would ease, only to erupt again and catch him off-guard later.

Sex just happened one night, six months after they'd set up together, marking a new phase of their relationship. When they finally made love, it wasn't anything earth-shattering. They were coy and gentle, playful and lusty, as they experimented with sex as a more mature part of their life together. At first, it seemed like another burden of commitment that neither wanted to embark on, each preferring the simple comfort of affection and moral support, but later it became a way for both to release tensions and express long suppressed emotional needs.

Seven months into the relationship with Dawn, Rick felt more confident and grounded. He decided to set up his own handyman business on the side and eventually become self-employed. Dawn was supportive and helped him make a business plan. Never had he felt so unconditionally and genuinely loved. But while he thrived in this climate, there were moments of intense irritation about Dawn's saintliness. If only she would complain occasionally or demand more attention for her own passions, he wouldn't feel so bad.

Over the next three years, Rick built a profitable handyman business with one employee and was feeling satisfied with his life, but his twenty-first birthday was spoiled when his mother brought her new boyfriend to the party. It made him think about marrying Dawn, but he wasn't thrilled with the idea.

Torn between his wish to run away from what he knew was the perfect relationship with the perfect woman and his need to be free, Rick buried his conflict by working longer hours so he could get a loan and put Dawn through journalism school; then, having done his duty, he would leave. Even making love to Dawn had become an obligation – until she came right out and faced him with the fact that he had lost interest in her. She asked what she had done wrong or could do better, but there was nothing he could fault her on. Oh, if only there was! It would be his ticket out without the guilt and shame he felt about being a heel like his dad.

They agreed to put the idea of marriage on hold until she finished school. The storm came in full force when Dawn got her journalism degree, just one month before she got a job as food writer and restaurant critic for a major online magazine. He felt like he had paid his dues, demonstrated his reliability, and proven to himself that he was not like his dad. Now he wanted to focus on his life, and he knew he couldn't do it if he stayed with Dawn.

One evening after dinner, Rick announced that he wanted to travel and devote more time to building his photography portfolio. As he spoke, Dawn grew increasingly upset and begged him to give her a chance to focus more on him, now that she was done with school. But Rick wanted to be set free from taking care of her, his mother, his sister, and anyone else who had claims on him. He needed to take care of himself, and the only way he could do that was to be unattached.

Over the next few weeks, Dawn's frequent meltdowns made it easier to leave, as he witnessed her losing her cool and finally putting herself first. Now he didn't have to feel like an ungrateful, heartless monster destroying his altruistic guardian angel. He did not feel eternally obligated to repay her for her devotion, so at age twenty-four, he sold his profitable handyman business, invested the money so he'd have an income to live off, and left Tucson to start his journey of exploration in the desert of Arizona. Of course, his mother and sister expressed disapproval, angry that he was taking off and abandoning them too. Instead of feeling guilty, Rick was keenly aware of their selfishness in wanting him as their 24/7, "go to" person, and he relished the thought of finally soaring free.

CHAPTER 20
FEAR OF INTIMACY – SIGN 6: DISCOMFORT AT RECEIVING COMPLIMENTS

"I suspect that you have some false belief in the virtues of misery and want to make your life martyrdom."

– George Elliot, *Middlemarch*.

Accused of being a "fake" on that cold, wet and windy morning in January made me feel as bare as the trees outside my office and as vulnerable to Rick's temper tantrums as those trees to the winter storms. Over the holiday period that ushered in the new year, I removed all the dead and twisted branches, twigs and leaves from the shrubs in my yard. Rick's journey in therapy seemed similar, as I cleaned out the old gnarled parts of his psyche, creating space for him to build a healthy connection with me in order to transfer it successfully to his wife.

I went on vacation for a week, joining a couple of friends on a coastal tour of the Baja peninsula, and for the first time in months I didn't feel Rick's presence invading my personal life. I bought myself ethnic jewelry and knick-knacks for the house. I discovered some rare herb seeds and took tons of photographs that later became the basis for my hobby of creating collages that soothed me during stressful times.

I returned to work refreshed and eager to find out how Rick had coped with the two-week break from therapy. I was taken aback in the waiting room when I saw a growth of fuzzy brown hair on his chin, but otherwise, nothing had changed. As soon as he entered my office, he launched into a tirade of complaints about how much he had suffered at the hands of his wife during the break from therapy. He blamed me for it, saying that I was not a "real doctor" because I had deserted him when he was going through hell.

"It seems you've come ready to do battle," I said, shocked.

"I complimented Christy like you told me to, but I got knocked down and felt like a fool. What's the use?" he said, looking away.

"You must have put a lot of effort into it, if you feel so unacknowledged."

"Her car broke down and I wanted to show her my admiration for coping all alone when it happened, but she trashed everything I said!" he scowled, folding his arms over his chest.

"It sounds as if you have been in the wars again," I acknowledged. "Why don't you fill me in on what made you feel so bad?"

Sign 6: Discomfort at Receiving Compliments

Rick sat upright and recounted the events leading up to feeling so inflamed, as a bulging blue vein pulsed on his neck...

Getting back to her part-time job as a librarian when Joel started school was something Christy both looked forward to and dreaded. But then the unexpected happened – her car broke down on the way to Joel's first day of school, and she was faced with an anxious child, a car stuck on the highway, and a cell phone with a dead battery! Somehow, amidst her panic, she hailed a motorist and used his cell phone to call for roadside service. Then she called Joel's school and her workplace to alert them to the delay. She sent Rick a text message about the incident and finally got her day back on track.

Rick texted back with concern and admiration for her as she rescued herself from the disaster. But by one o'clock, when Christy had not responded, Rick's anxiety got the better of him. He decided to call, this time offering to pick up Joel from school, but got no response. Rick made excuses for Christy in his head, telling himself she was too embarrassed to talk on her first day back at work, or that maybe she was still in shock about the whole incident. He decided to try to connect later, when they were alone at home.

That night, after Joel was in bed, he complimented Christy again about the efficient way she'd taken care of things while stranded on the highway. But Christy ignored his caring words, focusing instead on tidying up magazines and snack wrappers around the living room settee while rattling off the number of requests she'd received in the library for information on war games. He offered to take her away for a restful weekend break, but she changed the subject to Joel wetting his bed and misbehaving at school due to the trauma earlier in the day.

Rick felt gutted as she returned his compliments unopened. But then he had a flashback to all the times he'd wished he had persevered, when we'd discussed similar experiences in my office. He resolved to make one final attempt to connect with Christy, complimenting her yet again on her presence of mind and good parenting during the crisis. But instead of letting in his praise, Christy escalated her fears, imagining Joel developing a phobia about cars.

Rick felt utterly defeated. For the next few days, they argued about managing their schedules with only one car. Christy's lack of interest in joining forces so she could drop Joel at school and get to her new job on time made him feel as if he was being punished for his wife's unfortunate experience. She took care of things herself, shutting him out once again.

******

Rick sat up with a smug expression on his face as he concluded his story.

"You seem almost pleased that my suggestions didn't work," I said.

His face and ears went bright red as he whined, "It's not my fault!"

Sign 6: Discomfort at Receiving Compliments

"It's easier to bear if you can pin the blame on me, rather than feel that you failed," I observed.

He sat back, raising his eyebrows.

"You were brave to persevere with your compliments, despite it not working," I continued.

"I'm really worried that I'll have to live on the threadbare memories of the last few months," he said anxiously.

"I wonder if you heard me praise your efforts."

"I'm worried about the future of our marriage!" he snapped back.

"That's right, Rick. It's hard to take in compliments when you're scared about the future."

His head and neck sunk low into his sweater.

"Christy was trying to do the same thing you just did when I complimented you! She was gearing up to prepare for what might happen *after* the crisis she'd handled."

Rick froze for a minute and then made short, sharp, guttural noises.

"Do you know why it was hard for you to hear my compliments when you were scared?" I asked.

"It didn't feel right," he said slowly. "I wasn't *feeling* brave."

"So, if you're angry and scared, but I talk about your bravery, it doesn't fit, does it?"

He frowned and stroked his new beard.

"In this case, Christy actually made a connection with you by bringing you to the same emotional place she was in – one of fear. But it was jarring to you," I continued.

"I don't think this is helping me," Rick lashed out. "I'll just figure things out on my own, like I always do," he said scornfully.

"But isn't that what Christy says to you when you offer to help her?"

"I'm not like her!" Rick protested. "I don't push her away and build a wall around myself!" he yelled, clutching a cushion against his abdomen.

"The very fact that you think of yourself as more well-intentioned means that you separate yourself from her."

He slouched, releasing his grip on the cushion.

"What was it like to get Dawn's support and encouragement when you were antsy or worried?"

Rick sat perfectly still and stared at me. I held his gaze.

"It irritated the hell out of me!" he mumbled under his breath.

"What would you rather she have done?"

"I just wanted her to let me have my feelings," he said, collapsing into the back of the chair and pulling the pillows tight against him again.

"Okay, let's go back to the time when you tried so hard to praise Christy and make her feel good. What place do you think she was in?"

"She was panicked!" he said in a low, barely audible voice.

"How do you think she felt when you persisted in trying to make her feel like a hero?"

"Annoyed!" he said, now averting his gaze.

"Sounds like you feel ashamed because you're realizing why you failed," I said.

Sign 6: Discomfort at Receiving Compliments

He cleared his throat.

"When you try so hard to be perfect, you set yourself up for failure and shame," I explained.

"You always blame me and never say anything about Christy's faults!" he burst out.

"You're angry with me for showing you how you get yourself into these messes."

Rick looked away, his breath fast and shallow.

After a few seconds of silence, I nudged him: "Does this remind you of anything?"

"It's like the time when my mother let Beth off doing her chores but made me do mine because I was bigger," he said slowly.

"How did that make you feel?"

"Angry, jealous and resentful," he said, sticking his bearded chin out at me.

"So when you couldn't compete with Beth on age or cuteness, what did you do to get your mother to see how special you were?" I asked.

He was silent for a few moments, then perked up and announced, "I decided to be perfect!" as if he had just discovered the wheel.

"And what was it like when being perfect didn't work either?" I asked.

"I'd be angry that it didn't work, and then ashamed that I'd failed."

"So it's as if you've lost your battle to control your mother all over again!"

A few teardrops rolled down his cheek and settled on his upper lip.

"I don't mean to have battles. Why does it always end up this way?" he asked, banging the sofa arm with his fist.

"Well, is that really true? Didn't you have battles with Dawn in much the same way?"

Rick stared at a picture on my wall before answering. "No, things were pretty smooth until I just wanted out of the relationship."

"So what made that relationship less fraught with battles than your marriage?"

"I don't know. It was great at first, but then it got annoying, as if I were being squeezed into a shape that didn't feel like me," he recalled.

"So you fought for your individuality and your autonomy."

"Yes, exactly!" he said, nodding gratefully.

"Okay. So let's fast forward for a moment to you and Christy. Do you think she might be in the same boat?"

"I don't see how! It's not like we're mushed together and she's squirming to separate herself from me – it's the opposite!" he said animatedly.

"Talking about Christy's vacillating need for you seems to make you come to life," I pointed out. He blushed.

"Let's go back to your relationship with Dawn and compare notes. What do you think made it uncomfortable towards the end?" I asked.

"It got boring. She never put a foot wrong. Whatever I did, she understood and forgave. It started to grate on me." He paused and then asked: "So why did I end up having battles with Christy?"

Sign 6: Discomfort at Receiving Compliments

"You get to feel powerful by trying to make her want to be close with you. You also experience the highs when it works and the lows when it doesn't. That's far more appealing than the evenness and predictability of being with Saint Dawn!"

"My God, that's amazing! I felt my heart beat fast when you were talking about the excitement with Christy."

"Do you remember the thrill you felt when you first saw her?"

"Yes! It hit me like a ton of bricks – l was drawn to her like a magnet," he said in surprise.

"You sensed the excitement she offered. She wasn't going to be saintly and boring, but give you a run for your money, just like your mother."

"You mean I was attracted to her because she was like my mother?"

"Your unconscious recognized the similarity, and it attracted you. But this time, it was even more thrilling, because you had the power to make her respond the way you wanted – something you didn't have as a child," I offered.

"It's like something I have to do, but I feel like I just can't win."

"That's because you're using outdated battle tactics. Instead of having power struggles, like you did as a child, you can try to meet Christy as a peer in the here and now."

"I like the sound of that – being equal," he said eagerly.

"It's a two-step process: Step one: When Christy dismisses your compliments, stop it right in its tracks. Jolt her out of her auto-pilot mode and give her a reality check.

Say, 'Christy, I just gave you a compliment. You didn't acknowledge or react to it. What feels bad about it?'"

"I don't know if that will work," he said hesitantly. She'll probably get angry and feel accused."

"You've already dismissed the plan before trying it out! That's one way in which you set yourself up for failure, Rick."

"You don't know her like I do! I know how she's going to take this – I'm just being realistic!" he snapped back.

"Yes, you do know her better than I do, but your experience with her is colored by your expectation of failure and defeat."

He sank into his turtleneck sweater, looking down.

"No matter how often you fail to penetrate Christy's armor with your goodness, you persist in using it as your only tool of seduction," I said.

He winced.

"I'm giving you accurate feedback about your responses here, and if you do the same with Christy, there will be less hiding and more relating."

After Rick had another rant about why my ideas were useless, I called him out on the fact that he made Christy the obstacle, when in reality he didn't want to implement the strategy.

He poked his head out of his sweater, played with his beard, and glared at me.

I informed him that if Christy didn't react to the reality check that his feedback provided, he should tell her about the impact her anger had on him, in the moment. I explained that sharing feelings plants seeds of intimate

Sign 6: Discomfort at Receiving Compliments

connection and understanding. With regular watering, sunlight and food, those seeds germinate, sprouting roots that keep the relationship firm and supportive.

Rick sighed and complained about having to do more work.

"I notice you're ignoring all the rewards I've outlined for you, if you tell Christy about your reactions," I said when he'd finished.

"I feel burdened."

"I remember hearing that even in your darkest moments, you recalled our conversations and decided to give it another shot," I reminded him. "That shows how much you're benefitting from these sessions, even though you may not appreciate it now."

"I guess so. But it doesn't stay that way," he grumbled.

"Sometimes you'll hit a more perfect note, and other times it will be a noisy clash," I explained, as we ended the session.

******

Over the next six weeks, Rick vacillated between feeling confident and hopeless. At times he could hardly believe that sharing his feelings up front got Christy to come out of her shell. At other times he told me how strange and empty he felt without the constant marital battles.

Then, one morning, he came in very unsettled. He poured out his bitterness and outrage about the painful road towards intimacy, demanding that I make it smooth, easy and reliable – or else he would find another therapist!

CHAPTER 21
CHRISTY

"What we need is not the will to believe, but the wish to find out."

– William Wordsworth

A month after her CNN employers returned home, Christy quit her job. It was as if her clock had struck midnight, the ball was over, and her carriage had morphed back into a pumpkin. She couldn't reconcile being back on home soil in Taos with the part of her that had taken life by the horns and made the most of it in Europe. The voices in her head whispered that it was time to revert back to being the rejected, neglected, unloved child, whose job was to work hard and prove herself worthy of the prince who would one day find her and make restitution.

So Christy put away her natural exuberance and settled down to being a quiet working girl, just trying to get by. She had money saved up from her time abroad and used it to find a place to stay, buy a car and look for a job. She wanted to visit her parents, but decided against it, imagining that they would be critical of her time abroad as a nanny.

She spent time in the local library, looking for jobs online and filling out applications. Within a month, she saw a "help-wanted" sign in her local library and got a part-time job returning books, videos and DVDs to the shelves. In six months, her interest and extra effort with patrons paid off. She was offered a full-time position and help with tuition fees to attend night school to get her certification as a librarian.

It was so uplifting to be recognized and valued by Sharon, the chief branch librarian. Christy responded to the offer of sending her to school by taking as many classes as she could fit in. She dipped her toes in a bit of social life by having coffee with fellow students occasionally after class, then happily returned to her studio apartment, where she was alone and safe from the sexual needs that surfaced when she saw attractive young men. It was okay to be uninhibited and revel in the variety of sexual experiences she'd had when she was away from home ground, but in Taos, it was different. She felt she had to go back to her cage of self-deprivation, hoping it would somehow alert her parents to her need for them to beg her to return to their fold. Confined in her cage, she fantasized that her parents would sense her pain and come free her. She yearned to nestle in their loving embrace that she felt entitled to, and hadn't totally given up on. Masturbating was the only thing that took care of the dull ache of starvation for love from her family that no amount of books, work or study satiated.

But things changed overnight when, in her twenty-third year, she met twenty-eight-year-old Rick, who was taking a photography course at her college. They bumped into each other in the cafeteria when they both reached for the one remaining chicken salad wrap on the counter. Christy felt a jolt of excitement at his nearness. His gracious smile and invitation to sit with him swept her along as if she was walking on air. Rick was so attentive that she found herself telling him about the Moroccan spiced cous-cous dishes she had eaten in Spain and the Vietnamese Pho meat soups that had sizzled her palate in France. She gave him a buttery description of the Viennese pastries she had gorged on in Austria and talked about experimenting with Persian saffron in her meat dishes. By the time the twenty-minute class break was over, they had made a date to try out an ethnic restaurant after class the following week.

The next six days passed much too slowly. Christy found herself constantly thinking of Rick and imagining their date with a kind of fluttering impatience that was new to her. She had never felt this way about the boys she'd flirted with at school or the men she'd had liaisons with in Europe. In an effort to make sure that the threads of her cocoon were not unraveling, she loaded herself with double the usual workload each day, pushing herself to finish everything on time. After all, she dare not take the risk of letting her excitement make her vulnerable to the possibility that her expectations would be dashed again. Focusing on completing an endless list of jobs kept her safe from her desperate need for Rick to be the one to give her everything she wanted but didn't get from her parents.

When the day finally came, Christy tried to control the churning butterflies in her stomach by challenging herself with a complicated piece of research for her course on cataloguing, when she wasn't grabbing telephone calls and chasing after library patrons to meet and anticipate their needs. She flooded herself with activity – and it worked. Her mind didn't stray, and she won her battle to control her pressing need for the date with Rick to begin.

CHAPTER 22
RICK

"Children begin by loving their parents; after a time they judge them; rarely, if ever, do they forgive them."

– Oscar Wilde

Driving around the exquisite Arizona countryside for a year was invigorating and mind-opening. Never before had Rick felt so unencumbered and receptive to what life had to offer outside family duties. He started a travel blog where he posted his tales of adventure, wonder and amazement at the hospitality he received. Soon he had a growing band of online followers to update and share his life with. There were no expectations, no demands, no guilt, no shame, and no worries about being like or unlike his father.

He enjoyed having flings with hot women who were excited by his free spirit. The sex was sensual and uninhibited. It felt like the women wanted to enjoy physical pleasure as much as he did and were equally vocal in expressing their taste for adventurous sexual experiences. When he missed Dawn, he dredged up vivid memories of how he'd felt shackled by the sense of permanence she exuded.

Expanding his horizons by touring Nevada, California and Mexico for the next eighteen months was like filling his lungs with fresh air and exhaling all the past hurts, anxieties, traumas and failures. After so many new experiences, he felt clean and hungry for some stability that would allow him to create a life that combined both freedom and opportunities for growth. He had come to a point where he was ready to choose a spot to settle down and construct a framework for his future.

Rick's hankering for Taos, New Mexico, returned when the annual arts festival came around once again. He was drawn to the area like a magnet, to complete the journey he had taken the day his father remarried. Rick felt immediately at home in this world of natural art entrepreneurs. He fell in love with an old rustic cabin for rent and thoroughly enjoyed fixing it up. His handyman skills served him well and got him plenty of job offers that kept him busy for the next year and a half. Hotels and motels hired him to upgrade their facilities, and cafes and restaurants asked him to improve their outdoor seating arrangements. He got to use his skills as a photographer as well when tourist shops asked him to turn his scenic photos into postcards touting the area.

He went out on dates with single, divorced and separated women, but not one of them lit his flame. He still yearned for that effortless, seemingly eternal, reliable and fulfilling connection that he'd had for a short time with his parents before Beth was born. It had felt so right, but

Rick

no relationship since had ever come close to giving him that unique experience of contentment. Even now, when he was out and about during the day, his eyes would well up with tears when he saw fathers and their young sons buying camping gear.

A patina of sadness coated his waking moments, but he had no idea what it was about. He couldn't quite put his finger on that missing ingredient, without which life seemed insipid. He thought more and more about his mother and sister, and oddly enough he started having conversations in his head with his father. He wanted to know if his dad had felt as dissatisfied with life before leaving home as he was feeling now.

He wondered whether Jerry had found that special something with Wendy and whether it had all been worthwhile. He felt a jolt shoot through his body as he realized that he was actually identifying with his father. Immediately, he launched a huge counter-offensive by thinking of his abandoned mother and the sadness that had made her emotionally distant and often taken her away from him. But then he remembered her wily ways, how she'd wanted to devour him when she was empty and spit him out when she had a more varied emotional diet to choose from.

One morning, after weeks of feeling sad and unsettled, Rick awoke with an urgent need to see his family. It felt like he had to complete a mission that couldn't be ignored or delayed – an unshakeable force that he had to obey. He stuffed a backpack with a change of clothes and toiletries, jumped in his car, and set off for Tucson as fast as he could. The adrenaline in his system kept him awake and alert as he sped through the night, making it back to Arizona in record time.

With a bagful of bagels, cream cheese and orange juice, Rick greeted his sleepy mother at 6:30 a.m. in the house he grew up in. The reunion was clumsy, almost as if two old lovers were meeting again after one of them had found someone else. He felt like an intruder, no matter how hard Angela and her new husband Martin worked at trying to make him feel welcome.

In contrast, rekindling the relationship with his sister and getting to know her family was both heartwarming and addictive. The freedom to play with three-year-old Justin and two-year-old Kyle felt more invigorating than all the trips he'd made out to the wilderness. An old, rusty locked-up part of himself was unleashed, making him feel the limitless heights he could reach when there was no one to worry about, protect or take care of.

There was one more tug on his emotions that Rick had to attend to: seeing his father after almost thirteen years. He waited anxiously for Jerry to arrive at the café where they had agreed to meet. Strangely, he found himself wanting to hear about his father's life with Wendy, as if he were an old acquaintance catching up on his life story. At the same time, he couldn't stop the wronged son in him from wanting to harangue and punish his dad for all the pain and responsibility he'd heaped on Rick as a child. He wanted to make Jerry own his sins and beg for forgiveness. Rick came close to erupting with pent-up resentment, but somehow he kept himself in check. Only his hissing voice and piercing eyes gave him away, as snide remarks escaped his tight lips and he drowned in a tidal wave of sadness for the loss of the relationship he should have had with this pot-bellied, balding old man.

Gradually, father and son found some spots where the thorns of bitterness were less hurtful and exchanged information about their lives. Over that week, Rick saw that his father hadn't escaped the pain of leaving his family, just because he had Wendy in his life. He came to understand that Jerry, too, had suffered when Rick refused to have any contact with him. They acknowledged their mutual loss, but didn't go into the details. And although Rick couldn't forgive and forget, he allowed himself to have a dad again, albeit a failed one. The nagging hole in his heart was slowly healing.

CHAPTER 23
FEAR OF INTIMACY – SIGN 7: VIEWING CLOSENESS AS PARASITIC

"Your task is not to seek for love, but merely to seek and find all the barriers within yourself that you have built against it."

– Rumi

As spring arrived, I resumed my interest in collecting interestingly shaped leaves to make pictures and cards but it wasn't as satisfying as it used to be. I wanted something more alive and comforting, so I adopted a jet-black kitten who loved sitting on my lap and sticking his tiny head into the crook of my arm. It was a deliciously warm feeling, especially on those days when Rick ranted at me for not waving a magic wand and making his life blissful.

One Monday morning in March, he came in dirty and unwashed, with tiny crumbs in his now full beard, and a huge red pimple on his upper lip. His body odor made me step back as he brushed past me to get to my office.

Now You Want Me, Now You Don't!

He was bitter and angry. He wanted a better therapist, he said, who would make his marriage work, once and for all.

After the previous six weeks of getting on better with Christy, he had come unraveled again, and once again, *I* was on the hook. As he spoke, I had a flashback to a session three weeks ago when he had agreed to make a collage out of old magazines, depicting his experience of the marriage. He had been surprised by the elements of tenderness, stability and closeness portrayed in his picture. But now he seemed disconnected from those sensations – and from me.

My silent reflection of Rick's displeasure seemed to annoy him even more. "I think you *like* seeing me upset so I will keep coming to see you and keep your coffers full of money," he spat out.

"You think I get some sort of sadistic pleasure from watching you suffer?" I asked.

"Well, you're just sitting there, not doing anything!"

A knot tightened in my stomach, and I took a deep breath before saying, "That's how you must have felt when your father had an affair and no one did anything."

He stared at me, his eyes full of hurt, pain and rage. Then, in a low, angry voice, he told me about his bitter disappointment when Christy did not want to hear the good news he couldn't wait to share...

Rick secured a lucrative contract to do the photography for an online ad campaign that he had been trying to land for weeks. He called Christy as soon as he got the word, but she was busy at work and resented the intrusion. He was furious at being relegated to a non-urgent part of her inbox and thought of refusing the job just to spite her.

She checked in with him later that evening, ready to find out what he had wanted to tell her earlier. Doubting her interest, he gave her the news in a matter-of-fact way, crushed by her robotic words of congratulation.

Enraged by the situation, he imagined her tied to a tree, writhing as he shot her full of bullets, showing her how he felt when she machine-gunned his overtures towards her. Then he went to the gym, hoping to exercise his violent feelings into oblivion. By the time he got home, he was ready to wind down and try to sleep – and that's when Christy started to show an interest in his feelings. He recounted his success in an unemotional tone, only to be taken to task for not being more excited about his new contract!

At that point, Rick erupted with rage and accused his wife of trying to manipulate his emotions to suit her mood. Christy countered by saying that he was behaving like a spoilt child who didn't get what he wanted at the time he wanted it, then rejected it when it was available. Wounded by her insult, he reproached her for being unappreciative of the extra money his new job would bring in.

He slept on the sofa that night, hoping Christy would miss him and feel guilty about her hurtful words. But she didn't seem to notice that he had left the marital bed.

******

Rick's voice dropped as he finished telling me about this debasing experience. Then he raised his voice again, this time directing his anger at me for making false promises and taking him "for a ride." It became obvious that he felt our relationship to be as treacherous as the one he had with Christy.

"It seems like you want to snuff out any excitement I feel about good things happening between you and Christy, the same way she erased yours when you got the contract," I said.

"Oh, you're always sitting there on your high horse, making comments as if you know everything, and like *I'm* the screw up!" he said, sneering.

"You feel betrayed when the strategies I suggest don't work immediately. But that doesn't mean there's no progress."

"What progress? I've been at this for over a year and she still won't get close."

"Right now, you're denying yourself any positive thoughts or good feelings," I said.

"*I'm* not doing that," he shot back. "*I'm* not the one who has the problems in this marriage!"

"You have a problem with getting through to Christy so that you can be emotionally intimate in a consistent and stable way."

"*She* made this into a problem for me; I didn't have it before we got married."

"When you are so angry, you forget that you've been in this place before. Didn't you try to get close to your mother and fail? Didn't you try to get close to your dad

Sign 7: Viewing Closeness as Parasitic

and keep him in the family before he left all of you for Wendy?" I asked.

Tears welled up in his eyes. He shifted about, brushing the crumbs out of his beard, then quietly asked if we could look at the positives in the marriage. As we reviewed the fact that he and Christy now did more chores together, co-parented Joel as a team, and shared more about their pasts with each other, he relaxed and sat back on the sofa. Reluctantly, he agreed that when they exchanged their feelings in the moment, they enjoyed more intimate experiences.

"What is it like for you to have these small, intimate moments?" I inquired.

"Nice. But it doesn't feel like the big enchilada."

"I think that your expectation of a big, huge feeling of closeness prevents you from truly enjoying these moments," I observed.

"I can see that we share things more often," he conceded, "but it just doesn't feel like I'm in there with her emotionally and can stay there."

"What would that look like for you?" I asked.

"That she knows I exist and talks to me, and shares stuff with me."

"My guess is that you want something more. It seems that you want her to push everything else away and put *you* front and center."

"The way you put it makes me feel like I just want attention," he said.

"You were dislodged from your central place in the family when Beth came along, and when your father left for Wendy. So it makes sense that part of you is determined to get that special place back."

He retreated into the sofa. A large tear fell into his beard.

"Something I said touched you in a very sore place," I said. "What did you feel?"

"Relief," he said in a soft voice.

"Yes, it's relieving that there's a reason for the way you feel, and that you aren't just being a big baby," I acknowledged. "I wonder what feeling came next."

"I don't know… it was kind of gooey."

"Perhaps you felt my caring, and it melted your anger towards me."

Once again, Rick's eyes filled with tears. He sniffled and blew his nose, twisting the tissue in his hands before dumping it in the trash basket.

"It's hard for you to feel me as soft and caring when earlier in the session I seemed like a greedy monster using you to fill my coffers!"

"Is that wrong?"

"It's not right or wrong, but it means you are always having a fight with yourself about whether to think of me as the 'good" or 'bad' therapist."

"So?"

"Right now, you're experiencing Christy as the 'cold, mean wife,' so you don't take in the moments when she is caring and interested in getting close to you."

"I still don't get what I'm supposed to do differently."

"It's important that you notice the times when Christy seems indifferent and callous, so that you don't cast her in

Sign 7: Viewing Closeness as Parasitic

that role permanently and deprive yourself of her warmth, care and empathy when she is offering it. You need to jolt yourself into allowing for the possibility that she is also loving, interested in your feelings and wanting a connection with you, even though it isn't what you feel at that precise moment."

"Sounds awkward," he said, turning up his nose.

"It's not comfortable, for sure! But it's necessary so that you experience the other person as human – not all bad or all good, but a mixture, just like you," I explained.

"I just thought about how Christy does that to me! When she sees me as a monster, she doesn't remember the times when I was helpful or kind, and she pushes me away," he jumped in excitedly.

"That's a huge leap of progress for you."

We broke new ground as Rick allowed my praise for his insight to stand. For the next half-hour, we talked about the situations in which he felt comfortable being aligned with his wife, and the ones where he felt victimized or superior.

That's when he flew off the handle.

"You did it again! I was feeling so good, and then you started on again, telling me what I do that's bad!"

"So now I'm the monster again?"

My heart nearly burst out of my body when, after an interminably long pause, he finally looked at me and said, "I wanted to walk out just now, but then I realized that you are the only person who truly understands me, and I need that… I want it."

"You just achieved another milestone," I said softly. "You made a choice to go with your need for nurturing, instead of to that default victim place."

He smiled sheepishly.

We agreed to move on and discuss the hurt he'd experienced with Christy and zoom in on the moment when things went south. Rick drove right through the praise I offered and insisted on answers.

"Why did she shut me down when I called? And why didn't she show eagerness to hear how I'd landed the contract later that night?" he demanded.

"When you have a big feeling, like you did that day, she experiences you as a parasite sucking all her blood out and putting yours in there instead."

"That's ridiculous!" he exploded. "I just want to share a good experience with her – not take anything away!"

"What if we go back to what you wanted when you told her about your new job?"

"I wanted her to be over the moon and show it."

"Fine, but can you see that you wanted something big, all in one go?"

"Why is that big?" he asked.

"It's like you wanted to knock down her wall with one cannon ball."

"I still don't get it. The other people I told were whistling and yelling in celebration! Why shouldn't I expect the same from my wife?"

"Your friends and co-workers don't feel invaded or scared of big emotions. But Christy is already afraid that you will want more and more, so she has layers of armor to protect herself," I explained.

"How many more layers of armor am I supposed to fight my way through?" he demanded angrily.

"You're disappointed. But if you think about making millimeters of progress through that shield, then each tiny puncture along the way is a bonus."

He screwed up his face and leaned back on the cushions.

"But by the time she had dampened her sense of overwhelm and checked in with you about the good news, you had turned yourself off and responded mechanically," I continued.

His eyes darted towards me with a look of hatred.

"I'm the monster again, because I'm showing you that you were as cold as she was," I observed.

That set him off on another rant about how I was treating him as the perpetrator of the crime, rather than allying with him against Christy's cruelty.

"You want me to feel bad for not focusing entirely on you. Well, you put her in the same spot. She feels that she has to put her own feelings aside and concentrate only on you, or else she's a bad wife!"

"That makes me feel guilty," he said in a deep voice, his head bowed.

"Okay. Then maybe you can see why she has to wait until your emotions subside. She doesn't want that parasitic part of you to lay eggs inside her and grow."

"So how can I convince her that I'm not trying to take over?" Rick asked urgently.

"If you were Christy, would you want to face a tsunami of emotion or watch a gentle wave roll your way as it unfolds into something nice?"

"Obviously the latter, but I just don't agree that I am approaching her with a tsunami of emotion – that's not right!"

"Let me help you understand why it feels so different to her. Do you remember what it was like for you when you heard your father talking to Wendy on the phone before he left? Or when your parents argued while you were alone in your bedroom?"

"I was terrified and just wanted it to stop."

"It was a tsunami to you, but for your parents it was just the regular ups and downs of married life. Christy feels like you felt then."

He snorted and shifted around.

"If you give her the information about what's on your mind in tiny spoonfuls, rather than ladle the entire bowl into her mouth, it will work." I went on to give him some specifics hoping he would eventually sense my caring intentions. "It helps if you prime her by telling her what you'd like to discuss," I suggested. "Otherwise, she may go into panic mode and imagine all sorts of catastrophes.

"What if I have bad news?"

"It's the same principle. When you give her a context and the emotional tone of the information, like if it's exciting or alarming, she can sample it and see that at least it's not devastating or about to take up all her space," I explained.

Sign 7: Viewing Closeness as Parasitic

"Oh! I get it! *I* have to tone down my enthusiasm. Why should I have to change how *I* feel, just because she can't handle it?"

"Do you want her to join you and share your emotional life, or do you want her to be scared of your intensity and put up walls?"

"Obviously I want her to join me," Rick sighed, "but it doesn't feel right that I have to do all the compromising!"

"Remember the tool of feedback. You can tell her how frustrating it is to have to think so carefully about how and when you share news with her."

"It's hard to remember all these 'tools.' My head is swimming, and I don't know which plan to use half the time."

"Think about Christy *now* compared to how she used to be with you. That will keep your confidence afloat."

Over the next month, Rick was like a cat that got the cream. He was thrilled about Christy's positive response to the advance warning he gave her about any news he had to share. But how was she going to handle the news that he'd missed her terribly when she left for a week to help her sister, who'd just had her first baby?

CHAPTER 24
CHRISTY

"Love has its own instinct, finding the way to the heart, as the feeblest insect finds the way to its flower, with a will which nothing can dismay nor turn aside."

– Honoré de Balzac

Christy's first date with Rick went like a dream. He had eyes only for her, and she glowed with pleasure as she told him about her plans to become a certified librarian specializing in the history of global cuisine. She loved the fact that he didn't pry into her past or try to make passes as the evening wore on. For the first time in her life, she felt that she could enchant another human being just by being herself. By the end of the night, she felt special and desired – and she didn't need sex or masturbation to reach these heights of ecstasy.

Over the next year, she relished every moment with Rick. He took dozens of photos of her and the places where they ate, as they worked through their list of bistros, restaurants and native ethnic cafes. He talked about his dream of becoming a sought- after photographer for big-budget ad campaigns and his hope of getting assignments that took him all over the world. The affection they shared was supremely fulfilling to Christy, who finally felt satisfied and content with her life.

Rick was the most attentive companion Christy had ever had. He rarely asked anything of her except to let him make her happy by surprising her with new trips and discovering new eateries. But when he tried every now and then to start a sexual relationship, she resisted. She couldn't get enough of the affection and togetherness they shared and was fearful that sex would spoil it. Besides, she didn't need the sex, now that she had consistent, genuine love and affection.

Often they would relax after a movie and talk about their dreams. They both wanted a boy, a girl, a dog and a house in the country. Christy felt as if she were caught in a magic spell – she had found her soul mate! He was attractive, attentive and adoring. She could enjoy him when they were together, and then have her alone time to switch off and be with herself.

After ten months, Christy agreed to marry Rick, and they set about planning the wedding and finding a good location to eventually buy a home together. Six weeks before the big day, Christy holed up to cram for her finals. It was a relief to escape from the growing intensity of the relationship with Rick, who seemed to be claiming her as his possession and expecting more time together. While she was studying for her exams, she felt justified in ending their evenings early. But three weeks later, when she had passed her exams, she had no excuse. Now Rick seemed to want her around all the time, and it began to feel suffocating, making her alone time all the more urgent.

As the wedding day approached, Christy felt overwhelmed with the idea of her family being present. Would her mother's moodiness invade and intrude on her big day? Or would her mom put on her event planner hat and take over the whole thing? Would her father think she was beautiful and give her away with pride and sadness? Or would he just go through the motions, robbing her of the poignancy of the event?

Unable to shake her anxiety, Christy had sex with Rick many times in the weeks before the wedding, trying hard to control herself so that she didn't blow her cover as a demure "good girl" who did things the right way and at the right time. Rick seemed placated by her taking the initiative with sex, and stopped demanding more of her precious time to herself. And for Christy, the satisfaction of expressing herself sexually freed her from the agony of imagining how her parents might impact her wedding day.

Her family flew in from Los Angeles a couple of days before the wedding. Sonia fussed over Christy's hair, nails, shoes, bouquets and perfume. Her father told her how great it was that she had decided to settle down with a good man, and Sarah talked about how she'd missed her big sister. This sudden attention was seductive, and more than once, Christy fantasized about running off with them to live happily ever after in the idealistic family setting she had kept alive inside her all her life. But the afternoon before the wedding, her mother complained that the seafood at lunch made her sick. Once again, Sonia became the star of the show as everyone fussed over her, and Christy was relegated to understudy.

The hurt and disappointment felt oppressive. On the eve of the ceremony, she told her family she was tired and wanted a good night's rest, and to savor her last hours as a single woman. She masturbated with complete abandon, imagining that it would be the last time she would be in complete charge of her sexual pleasure and fantasies. For a moment, she felt the noose of "belonging to Rick" tighten around her throat and was tempted to run away. But then she thought of how adoring and understanding he was with her, so different from her scene-stealing mother at lunch that day. Her anxious heart calmed down when she pictured the house they were going to live in, beginning tomorrow, and all the fun she would have creating her garden and getting ready for the first child that she wanted to have right away.

Christy woke up excited and nervous on her wedding day. She was in a trance as her mother and sister fussed over her dress and veil, and her mind flitted between her father and Rick. Would her father make her feel like the most beautiful bride that ever walked down the aisle? Would he come through at the last moment and be the dad she'd always wanted?

The ceremony and reception went off precisely as planned, with Christy clinging to the image of her father's weak smile as he escorted her towards her husband-to-be. Then, all too soon, he was back at his wife's side. The second that her dad stepped back, after handing her over, brought a chill to Christy's bones, as if she was crossing a threshold with a sign saying "No return." But then she looked into Rick's eyes and allowed his love and joy to warm her soul.

On the way to the airport for their ten-day honeymoon in Hawaii, she talked to Rick about touring the botanical gardens, going scuba diving, and finding rare books for the library. She had begun her marriage with a ton of items to check off an ever-growing agenda, and it was just the way she meant to continue.

CHAPTER 25
RICK

*"Life as the waves make towards the pebbled shore,
So do our minutes hasten to their end;
Each changing place with that which goes before."*

– Shakespeare's Sonnets, LX

Rick got back into his routine when he returned home to Taos with a new spring in his step. He felt an enormous, gnawing space inside him, hungry for something more from life. He remembered the dream he'd once had of being a famous photographer, when his parents would claim him proudly as their son. It was time to take his photography seriously and make that vision a reality.

He had plenty of experience under his belt, but he wanted to give it the stamp of credibility, so he enrolled in a photography class at the local college. He was completely thrown off balance by having to relearn elementary things from square one, but he was encouraged by the positive comments he received about the portfolio he brought to class.

He met Christy at the cafeteria when they were both on break from their classes at night school. He found himself wanting to tear off the layers of coyness around her and uncover the pulsing seductiveness he could feel in his bones. They talked sensuously about exotic foods, as if they were already making out with their words.

On their first date, Rick felt as if he had known her forever. Their conversations about traveling and the cuisines of the world seemed effortless, and six months into their burgeoning relationship, he was keenly aware of the shot of energy he felt from head to toe the day before each date. It filled him with a sense of purpose that made him want to speed life up so he could entwine himself with her and feel valued and special. When they were together, it was as if he was exploring the world with a new set of eyes, ears, fingers and taste buds. It was as if Christy's sense of wonder when they went to offbeat, ethnic cafes rekindled the flame of pure joy he'd felt in his mother's presence, when they'd played in the park before Beth was born.

For the first time in his life, Rick was both physically and emotionally attracted to a woman, and he didn't quite know how to manage this twin desire. Christy seemed to lap up his physical nearness when he put his arm around her or his hand on her knee, but she resisted having sexual intercourse. He didn't want to push her into sex, despite his almost uncontrollable need to possess her. Photographing her on their weekend trips together was the only way he could keep his needs in check.

One late afternoon in the wild, as they patiently waited for a bald eagle soaring above them to land close enough for him to take the perfect shot, Rick asked Christy to marry him. He was elated when, after this nine-month courtship, she accepted his proposal. It was as if the seeds of hope he'd planted so many years ago had finally sprouted in well-prepared soil, producing the stem of a firm and bountiful family tree. After all, they were already on the same page about the kind of house they wanted, the number and gender of children, and their wish to stay close to nature. His dormant dream was about to be taken out of dry storage and reconstituted with the elixir of Christy's presence.

Once the wedding day had been set and the families informed, Rick wanted their lives to blend seamlessly together. Anything that took Christy away from him became a source of irritation, and he wanted to eliminate it in one fell swoop. He wanted to swallow this living, breathing vision of his dream before it disappeared or got grabbed by someone else. But he knew he had to bear the anxiety of waiting and distracted himself by getting his place ready for when she moved in after the honeymoon, as they still hadn't found their ideal house in the country. But just when Rick had resigned himself to waiting for sex, Christy suddenly initiated it a month before the wedding. He was shocked at her desire, but it was good to have this last gap between them bridged in a way that signified wholeness in their relationship. It calmed him inside, enabling him to relax and enjoy seeing his family members come together for his special day.

Angela and Martin arrived two weeks before the wedding and enjoyed the tourist activities Rick had planned for them until Christy's parents flew in. Jerry and Wendy came the following week, giving Rick a chance to get to know his dad again. He wished that he could enjoy this time of his life with both his parents together as a couple, but he settled for the peace he experienced by sharing his new life and professional portfolios with each in turn. On the few occasions when both his parents and their spouses were together in the same room, he was torn, drawn to his mother, sister and her children and feeling awkward that Wendy and Jerry were sidelined. His discomfort was eased as he and Christy enjoyed playing with Beth's kids together, confirming his expectation that she would be the perfect wife and mother.

The day before his wedding, Rick's emotions overflowed with incredulity and utter joy. Having his family around him, caring about his welfare and uniting around this important rite of passage in his life, meant everything to him. He acted as if his wretched past was a distant nightmare from which he had awakened. The memories of misery caused by his parents' bad marriage seemed like a wake-up call, strengthening his intention to be completely faithful, always available, and the constant source of his wife's happiness. He was going to make sure Christy's buoyancy was never extinguished so she would always be there to keep him effervescent and purposeful. He would fill her up with love and loyalty so she never needed to look elsewhere. And most of all, he was going to make sure that the bubble he created with Christy would never burst for lack of warmth, affection, and a closeness that made them melt into one another… forever.

CHAPTER 26
FEAR OF INTIMACY – SIGN 8: GETTING SICK WHEN YOUR PARTNER MISSES YOU

"The past, he thought, is linked to the present by an unbroken chain of events flowing out of one another. And it seemed to him that he had just seen both ends of that chain. That when he touched one end the other quivered."

– Anton Chekov

During most of early spring, Rick came to his sessions well-groomed and bubbly. His face would light up when I ushered him in from the waiting room, and he would begin by asking how I was or commenting on my clothes and jewelry. There were moments when he was aware that taking on the martyr role drove a wedge between him and Christy, but these times were short-lived. When he was on an even keel with his wife, he cast me as a judgmental authority figure, while he played the role of innocent victim. But when things were rocky between him and his wife, I was more of a savior he sought to rescue him from his undeserved plight.

The spiky nature of Rick's development was in sharp contrast to Ben's speedy growth into a big tomcat, out exploring most nights. Both Rick and Ben often kept me in suspense about whether they would return when they were both out doing their "male" things. I was as relieved when Rick came back to a session after threatening to quit therapy as when Ben got home late at night. Whenever Rick and I resumed our fractious relationship, it was like Ben allowing me to revel in his contented purring when he scratched at my blanket as I read in bed, falling asleep with him settling somewhere near my face, flicking his tail at me, chasing mice in his dreams.

In late spring, I had a dream about Rick almost drowning in an icy river current after his canoe turned over. I was watching from the shore, petrified that he would die. I yelled at him to keep his head above water while I called emergency services. I wanted to jump in and rescue him, but my feet were stuck in the frozen ground and I couldn't move. I woke up hearing his screams of terror as the current carried him away, but I was no longer scared. I knew he was going to be all right, that he would survive this crisis and become an expert at canoeing in dangerous waters.

The next time we met, he was scruffily dressed and antsy. I was relieved to see him alive, even though he had regressed to a state full of angst about Christy. He came at me with a booming voice, as if I was the sole cause of his hurt and exasperation. I listened with a racing heart,

Sign 8: Getting Sick When Your Partner Misses You

watching the veins in his head and neck engorge with rage as I became the target of his retribution.

I felt as powerless to help him now as I had in the dream. He blamed me for his relationship with Christy capsizing into icy waters and demanded that I rescue him. The lobes of his ears glowed red off and on as he gesticulated wildly. I asked him to slow down and tell me what had led him to feeling so upset…

Christy had gone to help her sister cope with the arrival of her first baby. When Rick heard her drive into the garage two weeks later, he gushed with relief that she was safely home. Then he poured out a torrent of fear that he had been harboring during their separation. He confessed that he had imagined her in a car accident, getting sick, or dying. He told her that the only way he could quiet his disaster-prone mind was to prepare himself for the worst – her death. As he went on about his concerns, he tried to get her to sit down, relax, and eat the food he'd prepared in honor of her return. Overcome by his own feelings, he had completely taken over, orchestrating the reunion in a way that gave her heartburn. Pushing away from the table, she escaped to the bedroom, ignoring his sad, confused look as she rushed to the safety of her bed.

It was as if his worst fears had been realized: he had lost his wife, and he was completely alone. He knew he had to keep an eye on Joel that night, as well as function as the man of the house with a sick wife. But all he wanted to do was crawl into bed beside Christy, hold her, and feel the warmth of her body against his. He wanted to smell her hair and warm her cold toes with his feet.

After spending one of the loneliest nights of his life in restless fits of sleep, he awoke to find his wife in a business-like mode, ordering him and Joel around, dead to his many attempts to check in and see if she was okay. As the morning wore on, his anxiety about their unhappy reunion spiraled into terror about the future of their marriage. Why had things turned out so badly? Why was it wrong to tell her he'd missed her? What on earth had it triggered in her that she had to punish him yet again?

******

Rick's chest heaved as he raised his voice in frustration, glaring at me as he demanded answers to his questions.

"You had an awful reunion with Christy, and now you want to have an equally bad one with me," I observed.

He pulled himself up, took a deep breath, and told me I was doing my usual mumbo-jumbo stuff with him.

"What was it like for you when I greeted you and listened to your upset feelings?" I asked.

"I don't know," he said, evading the question. "You tell me to be open about my feelings, and I was!"

"Your feelings were so strong that as soon as you got into my office, you let rip, as if there was no gap between the last session and this one."

He was dumbfounded, so I asked, "Were you bursting with pent-up emotions when Christy came home after her trip?"

He nodded his head.

Sign 8: Getting Sick When Your Partner Misses You

"Perhaps, when you're in that state, it's hard for you to remember that Christy may also have intense feelings and may not be able to accommodate yours at that moment," I noted.

"I just thought she'd be feeling exactly the same way."

"It's disappointing for you when she doesn't mirror your feelings. You wanted her to have the same feelings and experience them as strongly as you did. But it wasn't like that. So let's retrace our steps and see if we can find the point at which things started to go wrong."

I asked Rick what he'd felt about letting her go on the trip.

"I often wondered whether she would come back," he sighed heavily. "I imagined that she was enjoying her freedom from me and Joel," he said, nervously twisting his hands.

"You were very worried about this separation because she had chosen to leave you for her family, albeit temporarily."

"Maybe… It just made me think of when my dad would leave, and I never knew if he was coming back after one of his nights out with Wendy. I would be on pins and needles until he returned in the early hours of the morning."

"It sounds like you doubted Christy's commitment to you and Joel."

"I went back and forth. When she cuddled me the night before she left, I was over the moon. But then, when she let go of me so suddenly and left, I was decimated. It was like she gave me a life-line and pulled it back just as I was about to use it."

"What does that bring up for you?"

"Well, I never knew how my mother was going to be with me most of the time,"

"Can you see any connection between your confusion as a child and your confusion with Christy?"

"I don't think about those things when they're happening. If I have a feeling, I just go with it," he said defensively.

"When your mother let you down by going out with Beth and others, you felt like she was an angel who'd turned into a devil. You distanced yourself from her and, in effect, orphaned yourself. Now you are in danger of losing Christy if you continue down this path."

Rick lifted his head up, straightened his back, and looked me right in the eye.

"I saw Christy as a loving wife when she went away *and* when she came back, so I wasn't the one turning her into a monster. She made *me* feel like a monster, just because I missed her so much!" he said indignantly.

"Perhaps you didn't change your view of her, but you left an important piece out. What do you think that was?" I asked, nudging him along.

"I have no idea!" he snorted.

"Remember how you felt when you walked into the session today? You were so wrapped up in your big emotions that you left me out of the picture."

"So I did the same to Christy!" he exclaimed.

"When she came through the door, you were only in touch with *your* good feelings about your loving wife

Sign 8: Getting Sick When Your Partner Misses You

returning. You didn't pause to check where *she* was at, and then find a place where your emotions could meet hers."

"So I'm wrong again!" he exploded, hitting a cushion. "I was happy then, and I thought she was happy too. So why wouldn't she be okay with that?"

"But it wasn't just happiness, was it? You'd been imagining some pretty nasty scenarios too," I said, sitting back in my chair.

"That was before she came back."

"You cut off those fears and went with the joy. But they both still existed," I reminded him.

He looked dejected.

"Let's go back to the moment she came in through the door. Can you remember exactly what you felt?"

"Relieved! She wasn't dead or maimed or changed. Everything was going to be fine," Rick answered.

"Sounds like Christy's homecoming neutralized your anxiety. You weren't in touch with the excitement and joy of having her back – just your relief," I ventured.

"What are you trying to say? That I wasn't happy to see my wife?" he said, his face reddening.

"Relief blurred the happiness," I explained.

"I still don't understand. Why wouldn't she see that I was happy and relieved to have her back?"

"Imagine coming back and being given a blow-by-blow description of how tortured you were during her absence, and then how you had to deal with the worst fear of all – preparing for the worst case scenario: her death. How would that feel to Christy?"

"Probably a bit overwhelming."

"Destabilizing, most likely," I said. "And what happened to your fear?"

"It just went away."

"As a child, you were scared when your parents fought and relieved when they stopped. What did you do with the scary feelings?"

"They went away," he said impatiently.

"They calmed down, but they didn't go away. Perhaps you stored those feelings without understanding them, and then, the next time your parents fought, they were revived – and it was worse."

His face crumpled up into a pitiful image of ravaging, searing pain.

"The same thing happened when Christy returned home. Your fear was less obvious than the relief and joy. But she still picked it up, and it was overpowering."

"I don't understand. How could she pick up my fear when I wasn't afraid anymore?"

I felt his resistance to the idea of having contradictory feelings simultaneously.

"Do you remember what it's like when Christy is in a bad mood? It leaves its mark on you."

"Hmm…"

"When she came home, you felt better, but you transferred the acid of your anxiety to her and gave her heartburn. She was literally 'burned' by you making her so vital to your life that you would need to imagine her dead in order to cope with your fear of loss."

"I couldn't help it," Rick said, concerned. "I didn't mean to scare her. What can I do now?"

Sign 8: Getting Sick When Your Partner Misses You

"Right now, you guys haven't actually had a proper reunion," I told him, "So that may be a good place to start. What's the missing piece for you?"

"Hugging and talking."

"Perhaps you mean sharing more of yourselves with each other. You can ask her what it was like for her to leave and then come back. You can check in with her about what it was like for her when she opened the front door."

"But she won't talk to me now!" he said, getting agitated again.

A hint of annoyance crept into my voice as I felt him diminish every tool I gave him. "She *will* begin to tell you if you focus on specifics," I said curtly. Then I felt bad, and added, "For example, you can talk about how you thought of her during one of your favorite TV shows, or how you and Joel talked about playing a game with her when she got back."

"I feel so guilty now – like it's my fault I have taken us backwards."

Nothing I said seemed to comfort or nourish him, so I took a deep breath and tried this: "Every new setback is an opportunity to grow, and we can't do that unless we mess up."

"It's a hard way to learn!" Rick spat out.

"There wouldn't be much learning without the incentive to get past the pain of the here-and-now."

He fell silent, twirling a hole in the knee of his jeans. I felt sorry for him, but also furious that he seemed intent on destroying the value of what I offered before trying it.

"The best way to approach this is to do it in small bites," I explained. "Just throw out a bit of information about what you're feeling in the moment – like 'I'm glad you're back' – then let her take it in and respond before you tell her more. She might tell you that she missed you too. Then you can tell her about the times you missed her most, and she may let you know her experience of missing you."

"I just don't believe that she missed me! And I don't want to have to wait and wait till she finds that feeling and lets me know."

"You seem much more focused on your fears than on the possibility that you may connect and enjoy the reunion."

He shrugged, flapping his knees.

"Imagine Christy opening the door as she got home. Do you think she may have been anxious about your reaction?"

"Don't see why. She knows I can't wait to see her!"

"Maybe, but it doesn't mean that she doesn't wonder if you'll feel the same, or if you're mad at her for leaving you. After all, she knows how mad you were when your father left you."

"But that's not the same!" he protested.

"You feared that she would prefer her own family to you and decide to stay with them. So isn't it likely that she feared you'd be upset with her for choosing them? That might make her worry about whether you'd still want her back."

"I'm so scared that I can't think of her as anxious or worried. It's all I can do to deal with my own fears."

"But that gets in the way of you allowing two-way communication. You get so scared of hearing the worst

Sign 8: Getting Sick When Your Partner Misses You

that you make a preemptive strike by tuning her out. You've already decided what her response is going to be, so you don't check the evidence in front of you."

He cracked his knuckles and cricked his neck.

"You want to know that she missed you as much as you missed her, *and* you want to know she is equally relieved to be reunited with you. So you need to tune in."

He looked forlorn, as if I was suggesting the impossible.

"It won't come in just one burst and one exchange," I continued. "Brushing your teeth at night may have triggered a memory of you missing your bedtime routines together, and you can share that experience. Over breakfast, she may tell you what it was like for her to eat without you and Joel. That's how intimacy evolves, weaving the past and present together."

"Breaking it down into such small components just doesn't feel like closeness," Rick complained.

"Yes, it's hard if you approach it from an all-or-nothing standpoint. That's how you were brought up, but it doesn't mean that it's natural or healthy. Small, regular snacks of intimacy create long-term security. Then you won't have these wild swings between agony and ecstasy."

Now Rick was smiling. "That sounds like a good idea, though I'm not sure I'll like the evenness!"

******

Rick's next few sessions were steadier, and he reported that Christy had indeed been telling him how she'd thought of him at times during her visit with Sarah.

Hearing Christy tell him that she missed the sound of his breathing at night brought tears to his eyes.

Rick was feeling bad about the fact that he'd doubted Christy and his work with me, but at the same time things were looking up as his anxiety abated and he allowed himself to enjoy small but consistent moments of intimacy with his wife. He had a more positive outlook on the future – until one day, two weeks later, when he came in looking distraught and diminished. That morning, Christy had turned on him in the meanest of ways, making him feel like a piece of used chewing gum stuck to the sole of her shoe.

How was I going to get him back to feeling human again?

CHAPTER 27
FEAR OF INTIMACY – SIGN 9: DEHUMANIZING LOVED ONES

"When we argue for our limitations, we get to keep them."

– Evelyn Waugh

The beautiful May sunshine quickly disappeared as the Los Angeles "June gloom" brought dreaded dull skies and lower temperatures. My cat, Ben, looked wretched as he suffered with a nasty eye infection. He wriggled so much when I tried to administer the eye drops the vet had prescribed that I feared for his recovery. I tried to tempt him with his favorite canned foods and creamy milk, but he wasn't interested in anything but curling up and sleeping on the window sill.

As I sent birthday wishes to a cousin and aunt in early June, I thought of my father, who would have celebrated his eighty-seventh birthday later that month had a mysterious illness not claimed him quickly, six years ago. My mother had died of cancer in May, two years prior, followed by my sister exactly a year later. With mortality staring me in the face, I had traveled quite a bit after that to make up for all the years of study and internship I had undergone to become a psychotherapist. Suddenly, I felt an irresistible urge to return to Calcutta, my place of birth, and knew I had to take this journey in the near future. But how was I going to leave Rick for more than a couple of weeks at such a critical point in our work together?

My fears were realized when he came in for a session at the end of June, quiet and depressed. He seemed like a dried-up husk, as if his core had disintegrated.

"You seem worn out and empty," I observed.

"I don't care anymore. I am done."

"But you showed up today, so perhaps some part of you cares."

"My appointment was on my to-do list, so I'm just checking it off.

"Sounds as if you feel like a machine!"

"Yup," he said nodding his head.

"Can you tell me when you started to feel this way?"

"Not sure… a few days ago."

"What do you think triggered it?"

After a deep sigh, his voice cracked and he teared up. He cleared his throat a few times, grasping his sweater zipper, and then told me about his latest disturbing experience…

He'd heard Christy yelling at Joel for spilling mashed potatoes and gravy on the clean, white tablecloth. After the episode, she'd beaten herself up for being intolerant

Sign 9: Dehumanizing Loved Ones

and mean to her son, but no amount of understanding and comfort from Rick made her feel any better. Instead, she accused him of showing her up in front of Joel. Hurt and misunderstood, Rick had withdrawn and whisked Joel away from the ugly scene. But later that night, Christy insisted that Rick was the better parent and that Joel preferred him to her. Again, Rick tried to reassure her that she was a good mother and that Joel loved her as much as ever. But then she went even further and suggested that Rick deliberately played good cop, forcing her to play bad cop.

Rick tried to protect himself against her stinging accusations by switching off and becoming a block of ice. So it was a shock when, later that night, Christy reached out and caressed him, planting hungry, sucking kisses on his hands, his face, his shoulder, his chest, and pushing her body up against him. He didn't respond to her touches and moved her hand away when she tried to massage his genitals. He felt strong and powerful, resisting her expert foreplay.

******

There was no sign of that newfound empowerment as he finished telling me how he'd spurned his wife's sexual advances. Instead, he was slumped on the sofa like a wet rag that had just had all its moisture rung out.

"Did it occur to you that Christy may have *wanted* to turn you into a machine?"

"You mean she wants me to be robotic and uncaring?" he responded with disbelief.

"Christy was already beating herself up. Your softness and understanding threatened that process, so she had to depersonalize and dehumanize you, just like she'd done to herself."

"It's crazy that *I* have to be punished just because she wants to punish herself!"

"By doing to you what she does to herself, she's joining you together in a very intimate way, as if you are both one person," I said.

His mouth dropped open.

"Do you remember how you switched off your sexual responses so that she couldn't arouse you? Well, she did something similar, emotionally. She probably longed for you to tell her that she was still lovable, despite her cruelty to Joel. But she turned that tap off because she couldn't allow herself to be that needy."

"But I *told* her she wasn't a bad mother!" he interjected.

"Her need for reassurance became so huge that it frightened her. That's why she turned on you, accusing you of being perfect. It made her feel strong and in control again."

"So we're back to her not wanting to need me again!" he said sourly.

"What were you afraid of when you shut yourself off from her sexual advances?"

"I didn't want to feel weak and give in. It makes me feel like I'm dependent on her to make me feel good."

Sign 9: Dehumanizing Loved Ones

"So both of you are afraid of depending on each other and prefer to be in control."

"But I wasn't trying to control her! I was trying to console her."

"Yes, but in that moment Christy wanted to control her need for you to make her feel better. By depersonalizing both of you, she had no more human needs, and you had no human powers of comfort and care, so she was victorious."

"I hate these constant battles!"

"Then why do you keep going into battle mode, even though you tell me over and over again that you don't like it?"

"I don't start the battle. She does! I just try to stick up for myself… You told me to do that!"

"Rick, did you ever stop battling with yourself about avoiding contact with your father when he left home? Did you ever give up the battle to make your mother see your value and your worth?"

He turned his head towards me, looked down at the carpet, and in the saddest of voices said, "No!"

"No, you didn't want to lose yourself by giving in or giving up. It became a part of your identity. It's the same for Christy. She's doing battle with herself, not you."

We talked for a while about how awkward and unsatisfying it was for Rick to be at war with himself, because there was no winning. I pointed out how, nonetheless, in his mind, making Christy the enemy increased the chances of winning. He thought about that. "It felt so good to be the one rejecting her in bed that night, after the way she'd treated me and Joel," he confided.

"So you feel strong and powerful when you pay back in kind."

"Am I supposed to just let her walk all over me and use me as a toy?" he erupted.

"Paying her back like that may make you feel strong in the short run, but it makes you a pawn in the game of abuser and abused," I explained.

"I've never laid a finger on her!" he yelled, his face going red and his eyes bulging.

My mouth went dry and my heart raced. I felt as dehumanized as he'd made Christy feel, and it was a while before I could speak. "When Christy reacts with venom to your attempts at consolation, she is the emotional abuser and you are the abused. But it works the other way too: When you choose to be deliberately cruel by refusing sex or not responding to her attempts at reparation, you are the abuser and she is the abused."

The air was heavy with unspoken emotion. I knew I had to put his feelings into words so he wouldn't drown in his turmoil. "I imagine you loathe yourself for being cruel like Christy and, worst of all, you think I must hate you – just like you hate yourself."

Rick nodded and turned his face away from me in shame.

"I understand how bad you feel, especially when you try so hard to be a good, loving person."

"But I'm not, am I! I'm vindictive and sadistic and just want to pay her back for all the hurt she has caused me."

Sign 9: Dehumanizing Loved Ones

"When you're full of self-loathing, you want me to beat you up. That's what Christy wants too. You even wonder how I can still bear to have you in my office and speak to you. Well, those emotions are similar to what Christy was feeling," I pointed out.

He shot me a glance, then fixed his gaze on the bookshelves to his left. He seemed to be deep in thought. I checked in with him after a minute or so.

"You seem to want to figure this out on your own, when we could do it together."

"I don't get why she thought sex could mend things between us," he said slowly.

"By the time you were in bed that night, she was terrified that she had totally alienated you and tried to undo it by having your bodies do the making up."

Again, a long silence. He glanced at me sideways and saw that I was still intently focused on him. "You're surprised that I am still with you," I said gently.

"I am surprised," he said.

"But I bet it's comforting and reassuring."

"Yes, very," he agreed. "I don't feel so bad now."

"Why do you think that is?"

"You made it okay for me to feel cared for, even though I was ashamed and disgusted with myself."

"Yes, that's the basis of empathy. When you can accept that, you are just the same as your loved one, and you don't have to resort to power, control or abuse in order to feel worthwhile and strong."

"I know that," he said with irritation, "You've told me this before. But when I tried to be empathic, she killed me off!"

"You allowed her to kill you off! You could have seen yourself as stable, helpful and caring, but you gave *her* the decision-making power," I said.

"How can I avoid doing that when she chops me up?"

I shifted around in my chair, thinking of how to word my response in a palatable but impactful way.

"You need to give her a clear message that she can't switch you off and on to suit her mood. Then you walk away, staying tuned into your emotions."

"But that sounds selfish! What if she hates me and stops connecting completely?" he asked anxiously, playing with the ring on his sweater zipper.

"You can be assertive and protect yourself without having to battle for power."

"So what should I say when she's in one of those self-hating moods?"

"Tell her that you feel rejected, sad, or angry at being turned into a monster, or disappointed that she refuses your comfort – or any combination of the above. It will stop her in her tracks and remind her that you are a human being with feelings. Then give her a choice. Ask her if she wants to flog you both, or if she wants to receive comfort and understanding."

"That sounds good. But I don't know if I can remember to do that when she attacks me."

"When she feels you as solid, no matter what mood she's in, she will feel safer and won't need to attack you."

Sign 9: Dehumanizing Loved Ones

Rick worried that putting up personal boundaries and being his own man would create an even wider distance between himself and his wife, making them into separate individuals, rather than a close couple.

So we reviewed the past eighteen months and discovered that he'd been equally dubious each time I'd suggested adding a new string to his bow. But in a short space of time, he was implementing these ideas routinely.

As we focused on his successes, his face lit up and his life force returned. I commented that his successes hadn't fully registered until we'd reviewed them together. I also pointed out that he focused more on the bad than the good stuff, making the latter less rewarding.

He raised his eyebrows in amazement, "So, I don't see the intimate moments at the time they happen, and then I think there aren't any!"

"Precisely! So how can you be more mindful of those moments as they are occurring?"

"I don't know. They seem so small and disappear so quickly," he responded, looking lost again.

"What if you kept a little notebook of those moments when you feel close and connected with Christy and then reflect on how it happened? You can rewire your brain to attend to the positive moments in your relationship, just as Christy is rewiring her brain to feel safer and let down her guard."

"Okay, but it seems like a lot of work," he said despondently.

He looked tired and sad, but I felt it necessary to stay with the theme, to show him that just as I was persevering with him, he had to do the same for himself.

"It *is* a lot of work, because you have to deliberately focus on her loving intentions, rather than stay on auto-pilot and sniff out the negative ones," I said. "But it's necessary, if you and Christy are going to see the caring side of one another on a more consistent basis and make *that* the default position of your marriage."

"I just don't know where I'm going to get the energy from."

"How did it feel earlier, when you felt me caring for you, even though you didn't think it was warranted?"

"I felt lighter and better about myself."

"I notice that when you allow yourself to accept my care and commitment, you're full of energy and motivation. But when you fight me or get suspicious of my motives, then you're running on empty and everything becomes a tireless job with few rewards."

Rick's cheeks and ears went red instantly.

"See?" I said. "You want me to care, no matter how down you are or how much you resist me – but you don't want to need it. Just remember that you and Christy are in the same boat on this one."

This time he grinned with acknowledgement that he had been well and truly seen!

"Okay, that's the first good moment I will write down when I get out of here!" he remarked, bright eyed and bushytailed, showing me that he was aware of the good stuff between us in that moment.

Sign 9: Dehumanizing Loved Ones

I wondered how long he'd hold onto this pleasant banter between us at the end of the session. Would he just taste it and spit it out? Or would he breathe in some of the vibrancy he'd gained from our interaction and share it with Christy, passing on the baton of life's potent energy?

CHAPTER 28
FEAR OF INTIMACY – SIGN 10: USING ANXIETY TO KEEP LOVED ONES AT BAY

"How can a woman be expected to be happy with a man who insists on treating her as if she were a perfectly normal human being."

– Oscar Wilde

Over the hot and dry summer, my cat, Ben, got over his eye infection. He was out and about again, bringing dead frogs and birds to my back door. Meanwhile, I was diagnosed with a tumor in my uterus that was due for surgical removal in late October. As I harvested the leeks, cucumbers, broccoli rabe, and fava beans from my garden, I wondered whether I would live to see my newly-planted lily bulbs bloom next year. Would I get to take my trip to Calcutta booked for May? And how would Rick react to me leaving him twice within seven months?

Preparing Rick for my upcoming surgery without divulging the reason wasn't easy, but I gave him two months' notice so we could process his reactions. I expected that it would trigger him in the place where he had been hurt by parental abandonment. If so, we could do a lot of important work around it; if not, then I'd know that he wasn't ready to deal with this crucial issue of separation from a caring person in his life.

At first, he indicated that he would welcome the break. Then he started to arrive late and cancelled a session at the last minute. When I saw him again, he railed against his lack of ability to control me and accused me of putting my health before his emotional needs. We talked at length about his feelings of not being important and his rage at feeling disempowered. He calmed down considerably after each of these volatile sessions, realizing that I wasn't running out on him, even though it felt that way. After these stressful meetings, I would seek out my best friend and confidant to help me feel like I wasn't being "a bad mother," like Angela, to Rick.

A week before my surgery, Rick arrived looking like a nervous wreck. He was terrified that he had irretrievably jeopardized his marriage, and that I would throw him out of therapy because he hadn't used the strategies I had offered on a regular basis.

Looking tense and afraid that I would be mad at him, he started talking at a fast and furious pace before he sat down, repeating himself and losing his train of thought.

"I haven't seen you so frightened since we first started working together," I began. "Are you worried about whether I will come back to you after my surgery?"

Sign 10: Using Anxiety to Keep Loved Ones at Bay

"I hate this! I don't want to care about you, and I don't want to care about not seeing you for the next three weeks," he said, choking back tears of rage.

"I'm sure it makes you feel like a helpless child again, and that's awful," I acknowledged. "How would you like things to be?"

"I want to manage on my own and not feel like I need you."

"Then you'd never have to feel let down, unimportant or abandoned when someone you depend on has to take care of themselves for a while," I interpreted.

Two large tears fell down his cheeks as his shoulders sunk down into the sofa.

I thought back to how difficult it had been for Rick to tell his wife about his fears of their separation when she went to help with her sister's first child. Out loud, I remarked on the progress he'd made by sharing his anger and fears before I left, rather than later.

He received the compliment without letting it comfort or reassure him. Instead, he changed the subject, going straight into talking about the tensions between him and Christy.

"A couple of days ago, she asked for my help with a family dinner we had planned, and I was over the moon that she wanted me. Then, the other night when she couldn't sleep and I asked what was bothering her, she bit my head off. She made it clear that she wanted to deal with things on her own, and that it was my nagging that made her anxious. I felt rejected and useless again," he spilled out, hardly stopping to take a breath.

"That's exactly how I feel now!" I said. "You don't want my help, even though you told me how scared you are of being alone while I am gone."

"You think I come here and pay you a fortune for a piddling amount of time because I don't want your help?" he raged.

"Right now, you want me to be inhuman so you don't have to need me as I get ready to leave you."

Rick squirmed and opened his mouth to deny it and fight me again, but in the next second he stopped and said: "I am scared."

"What's scaring you at this moment?" I asked gently.

"I'm scared that you'll be so relieved to have a break from me that you won't want to work with me again," he said, looking down at his scuffed loafers.

"What makes you so awful to be with?" I asked.

"I wonder how you can put up with me when I treat you as inhuman and get so angry all the time," he said haltingly.

"Perhaps you want to upset me so that I will dismiss you. Then I am no longer in the picture, so no need to worry about losing me in surgery."

He pulled a cushion up to his chest and buried his chin in it. "I want you to care now, but I don't want to care about you when you're gone," he mumbled.

"What was it like when Christy snubbed you for trying to help with her worries?"

"She told me I was making things worse and that she was better off taking care of herself!"

Sign 10: Using Anxiety to Keep Loved Ones at Bay

"Isn't that what you're telling me today, as I try to help you with your worries about our separation?"

He raised his eyebrows and stroked his beard.

"Do you think you can understand Christy better now?" I asked.

"I suppose so, but it's hard to connect the dots."

"What happened to our connection when you rejected my help with your fears?"

"We stayed connected," he said, shocked at this revelation.

"So, even though we were in a bad place, we were able to connect and stay connected," I noted.

"I still wonder if you will be happier not seeing me when you are off work."

"Sounds like you don't feel our connection will last."

"Yes, that's exactly how it feels – that it can crumble in the blink of an eye."

"What happened to the intimacy we just shared a moment ago? Has it crumbled in the blink of an eye?" I queried.

"I don't know what you mean!" he protested.

"We'd just acknowledged that, despite your fears and my feelings of being unwanted, it brought us closer. I wonder what happened to that closeness."

"I don't know. I felt anxious again."

"My recollection is that when I praised you for sharing your anger in a more mature way, you ran from it."

"Hmm…" he mumbled.

"Something about us being intimate in that moment scared you. Perhaps it was because I recognized your growth and ability to cope."

His face turned red and he became quite agitated. "I knew you were telling me something good, but I didn't like it."

"You were angry at me for choosing my health over you. You wanted to make me feel guilty about it, but you couldn't continue with that plan when I labeled your anger 'mature'!"

Rick examined his phone several times before returning to our conversation. "It felt like you took something away from me," he said quietly.

"So you feel empty if I show you that you can manage because you're more grown up now."

He hid his face in embarrassment.

"You want to make up for all the times you hid your anger and fear when your parents left you. But if I praise you for acting in a grown-up way, you feel that you no longer have permission to show your anger."

"I felt you wanted me to just accept that you're leaving me and not make a fuss."

"What would you have preferred me to do?"

"Tell me that you won't have surgery," he said.

"Maybe you feel we are competing for a finite amount of care," I offered. "If I care for myself, then I can't care for you."

"That's how it was for me!" he said defiantly. "I cared for my mother and sister, not myself. And I do the same with Christy."

Sign 10: Using Anxiety to Keep Loved Ones at Bay

"So someone always has to sacrifice themselves to make a relationship work?"

"If you put it like that, I guess so," he said calming down.

"When you and I were open with our feelings, you were initially relieved, but then you got scared. What were you frightened of?"

"I didn't want you to see any more stuff about me. I wanted it to be about you."

"It's the same fear that's popping up for Christy. She doesn't want you to see through her. She wants to keep some parts of herself private. When you try to see it all anyway, she shifts the focus onto you and your nagging."

He shrugged and took a big sigh.

"Think back to how she saw you as a greedy monster when you tried to be the center of her world. That fear is now coming back to fill the space that was taken up by the shields, walls and other defenses she dropped as you both got closer."

"Oh, so we're back to square one again!" he said with a mixture of rage and dejection.

I didn't respond.

"What! Why are you silent?" he demanded.

"It seems like you're rejecting anything I say that doesn't match with your determination to make Christy the villain," I said coldly.

"I hate hearing all this stuff about her fears and I don't like hearing about my stuff either. I just want everything to be okay, and to not have to work at this anymore!"

"That's honest. But look at the state you were in today when you came into the session. You were terrified about me leaving you and needed me to understand, be patient, and care for you, despite the fact that you had regressed. That's what happens at Christy's end too."

"So what happens now?" Rick asked, clearly frustrated. "Do we have to go through the entire cycle again until she stops being scared?"

"It's a different experience of fear for her, because this time it's coming after enjoying a closer and more intimate connection with you. And it's also a different experience of frustration and fear for you because you've achieved longer periods of closeness, and it hurts more when that gets ripped away."

"But what should I do if she suddenly withdraws or rejects me after letting me get close?"

Controlling my frustration at his continual focus on "what ifs," I answered, "Before you and Christy got close, she had only bad memories of relationships. Now that she's tasted a more positive connection with you, she's at a crossroads. Should she trust in her recent experience of intimacy with you, or go with her more familiar past?"

"But what am I supposed to do while she goes through this conflict?"

"Maybe you're facing a similar conflict?"

"Well, I suppose I don't know whether to trust that she'll be warm and affectionate, or fear that she'll be cold and rejecting!"

"Can you recall the anxiety of not knowing which image of Christy to go with?"

Sign 10: Using Anxiety to Keep Loved Ones at Bay

"Yes! I remember being really torn, looking for clues but not finding any. Then I get more anxious, and it becomes quite chaotic in my head."

"That's how Christy was feeling the other night. Sometimes you feel inviting to her; other times you scare her. So at the very moment when you tried to comfort her and share her problems, she experienced you as a scary intruder and reacted accordingly."

"It feels like no matter what I do or how hard I try, no matter how patient I am, she's always going to have this fear – and there's nothing I can do about it."

At that moment, I wanted to yell out that I felt exactly the same with him. But I kept my composure, saying instead, "You feel like she's going backwards and dragging you down with her. But what I notice is that you spiral down really quickly when you sense her closing the door, and it's hard for you to pull yourself out of it."

"Well wouldn't you feel the same if you'd worked so hard and for so long, and thought everything was going according to plan? And then, *boom*, it's back to the way it was before!"

"You see that as a permanent loss, rather than part of a learning process."

"So now it's *my* fault again!"

"Blame is not the issue here," I said, feeling tested once more.

"It's the same pendulum that swings for both of you, but it's not swinging as violently as it used to. You are just not fully aware of the change of tempo."

Rick seemed more subdued. "So what now?" he asked.

"You are both anxious, and that makes it difficult for you to empathize with each other, but you can ease the anxiety through touch. When you are aware of Christy's tenseness, you can gently touch her back, hand or shoulder. It's a way of acknowledging that you get where she's at and that you're in a similar place."

"But what if she pushes me away and tells me not to touch her, because that's what she did when I asked her if she was okay?"

"Asking her is more intrusive. Touch releases bonding hormones that reduce anxiety and stress."

"I'm not sure whether she'll take it that way," Rick said, "but I'll consider it."

"I know you don't want to get rejected again. But your anxiety about getting pushed away is a bit like Christy's fear of you grabbing her emotionally 'free spots.' The fear keeps you stuck, anticipating the worst."

"It all sounds so easy when you describe it, but I'm not convinced that I can get through to her and stay there."

"It's not an all-or-nothing situation. There will be times when she'll let you in all the way, and other times when she'll barely open the door. Just like you don't always feel like playing with Joel or taking a call from a client."

I sensed that he wanted to prolong the session and was interjecting his doubts in an effort to get me to stay with him longer. I wanted to call him out on the fact that he was fighting with himself over wanting more time with me and not wishing to want me at the same time; but I also just wanted the meeting to come to a close and recharge my batteries.

Sign 10: Using Anxiety to Keep Loved Ones at Bay

I reminded him about the contingency plans we'd made if he had a crisis while I was gone and listened to his protestations that he didn't need a babysitter or a substitute therapist. Relief washed over me as he left the office, but later I felt guilty for wanting to focus on my surgery five days away. I also began preparing myself for the possibility that Rick may not come back to therapy when I returned to work. He might retaliate against my leaving him by abandoning our relationship prematurely.

CHAPTER 29
MOURNING THE PAST: FACING INTIMACY SAFELY AND SECURELY

"We cannot change anything until we accept it. Condemnation does not liberate, it oppresses."

– Carl Jung

The tumor in my ovary was benign, but I suffered post-operative complications that kept me in hospital for over two weeks. My delayed recovery meant that I had to tell Rick I would be away for an extended period of time. He didn't respond to the first two calls I made. It felt like he was giving me the cold shoulder for leaving him for longer than expected. He returned my third call as if I was a nuisance he could no longer ignore. Reluctantly, he agreed to resume his regular sessions the following week.

He was formal and guarded when he came in that December day, as if we were meeting for the first time. It was obvious that he had closed up again and was uncomfortable letting me back in. He gave me tidbits of information about his son starting first grade and his wife's successful online sweater business. Otherwise, he claimed to be doing fine – until I asked about how he felt when I had to extend my leave of absence.

He started off saying it was no big deal, but I heard that familiar crack in his voice that suggested there was more to it. When I commented on the change in his tone, he crumbled and told me how scared he had been for my life. He'd been worried that I would disappear before he had finished the job of developing a stable connection with Christy.

This was the breakthrough I'd been hoping for. At last, Rick was acknowledging missing an important person in his life in a way that opened the door to mourning: mourning the loss of his idyllic childhood before Beth was conceived; grieving for the father he'd lost to Wendy; mourning the loss of his childhood when he became the parent figure to his mother and sister; and finally, mourning the loss of his vision of the perfect union with Christy. Now he had room for a rich, deep and fulfilling relationship with his wife.

Over the next few months leading up to my trip to Calcutta, Rick and I discussed how he felt about me leaving him again. This time around, he was able to share his anger at me for going away so soon after the last break. He also talked of his dread that I might never come back. Each time his anger or fear was aroused, we traced it back to a similar childhood experience that had been pushed aside and left to rot in a fetid pile of traumatic emotional memories. He grappled with his rage, then slowly dug the pit that would hold the remains of these mummified experiences.

A series of dreams Rick had during this period proved to be crucial in understanding his strong wish for a perfect fairy tale relationship with Christy, and how unrealistic that was. As we analyzed these dreams together, he seemed to get stronger, gaining a sense that he was the author of his own experiences. I could see this was setting the stage for him to throw off his victim persona.

By the time I left for my long-overdue trip to Calcutta in June, Rick was not only able to express his sense of loss, but also a sense of deep longing for the time when we would reconnect.

When we resumed our work together three months later, a newer, more mature version of Rick seemed to emerge as he settled into therapy. At first he indicated that he had coped well and was proud of himself. But over the course of the next few weeks, he began to disclose that he'd missed our sessions. He mentioned that he'd coped with the feelings of loss by dialoguing with me via his journal. He had kept me with him in a way that brought the relationship to life, even when we weren't physically together.

******

Rick and Christy started couples therapy in December of that year, just shy of the third anniversary of their first aborted attempt. Both seemed safer in the knowledge that they had survived seven rocky years together, making it less likely that either one of them would walk out on the other. Rick was seeing Christy more as a human being with shortcomings, fears and needs, just like him. His therapeutic journey had given him the care, love and security he needed to feel wanted, despite his imperfections. Now he was ready to do that for his wife, safe in the knowledge that he had sound and reliable support from me. He'd proved his commitment to Christy by being willing to examine his role in the problems between them. This made her less afraid of being cast as a demon and more willing to trust in his steadfastness. She asked to join in the therapy, wanting to take a more active role in the conversation.

As they came to the sessions together, they began to develop a vocabulary of emotion that allowed them to share their experiences and feelings without having to put each other on the spot, demanding proof of love or loyalty. After just six months, I could see that Rick and Christy were finally on the road to feeling secure, building a flexible house of intimacy along the way.

AFTERWORD:
HOW THE SEEDS OF FEAR GET SOWN AND INTERFERE WITH THE CAPACITY TO BE EMOTIONALLY INTIMATE

"In consequence, there were good seeds from good plants and bad seeds from bad plants. But seeds are invisible. They sleep deep in the heart of the earth's darkness until one among them is seized with the desire to awaken. Then this little seed will stretch itself and begin – timidly at first – to push a charming little sprig inoffensively upward toward the sun."

– Antoine de Saint Exupery, *The Little Prince*

Growing up in a home where people don't share their day-to-day feelings means that everyone stays in the dark about what's going on for one another. Emotional experiences are treated as if they don't exist. Young children learn to shut off their feelings in order to survive within the family. They become skilled in bursting their bubbles of neediness when they surface, preferring instead to be armor-plated and safe. Parents have no idea that by discouraging emotional expression in the family, they are hindering the ability of their children to form intimate connections later in life. They probably had similar experiences in their own childhoods and regard this as "normal."

Young people brought up with the message that emotional connection is taboo feel there's something wrong with them for desiring emotional intimacy, and they often develop shame around any sign of neediness. They come to think of their normal, healthy need for closeness as wrong – if not downright dangerous – because reaching out for it may bring ostracism from the family.

Parents or other family members may unwittingly reinforce this sense of isolation by connecting with their children's attributes or accomplishments – appearance in the case of girls and skills or achievements for boys – instead of with the whole person. When their emotional experiences are shunned or stifled, children develop an unhealthy discomfort with their feelings, ruining their chances for successful intimate relationships as adults.

Encouraged to "be a man," boys strangle the need to understand the intense roller coaster of uncomfortable feelings that come up in childhood. They dismiss these emotions as raw sewage, preferring the sweet-smelling attention they can rely on for being strong. They're praised for rescuing others from physical danger and for taking care of family members by fixing things around the house. Bodily strength and endurance are ideals they are pushed to emulate at the expense of their emotional growth. Often, helping family members deal with problems or logistics when they are stressed earns them the admiration of their parents.

Parents usually make things worse by focusing on their own needs instead of those of their children. A mother who prizes her son for his handsome looks and caretaking potential may send a double message. On the one hand, she's delighted that he's attractive to other women, but on the other, she feels a kind of possessiveness, wanting to keep him for herself because he's her creation. This confusing message evolves into a code of silence, preventing her son from making a smooth transition to adult relationships beyond the mother-son connection. All too often, there is no conversation that allows the young man to resolve his emotional conflict around establishing a new romantic relationship outside the family. Thus, the vital differentiation between intimacy with a mother and with a partner is never addressed.

Torn between their natural inclination to mate with another woman, both physically and emotionally, and the possessiveness of their mothers, men in this unenviable situation often split themselves in half – they stay emotionally loyal to their mothers while courting their partner, until they can no longer tolerate the conflict and feel the raging need for emotional intimacy in their romantic relationships. But by then, they are up a creek without a paddle, desperately flailing around for a way to calm their inflamed yearnings. At this point they attempt to woo their partners into a more emotional connection by using romance and sex, but fail miserably to achieve their goal.

Fathers, too, can give their daughters confusing messages about intimacy. By commenting primarily on the beauty and charm of their adorable daughters, they elevate the power of physical attractiveness to win attention and love. Young girls who are adored as "daddy's little princess" and showered with kisses, cuddles and words of admiration for their beauty, come to think of themselves as attractive and desirable, entering womanhood with enhanced self-esteem and confidence based solely on their appearance and sexual magnetism. Used to being the apple of their father's eye, they may experience a gnawing emptiness that becomes magnified when they no longer get the same response from their date or mate to their seductive charms. Suddenly, they become acutely aware that they don't feel as connected with their partners, causing them to focus on improving their looks in order to pull them back into an intimate embrace – as if they could rewind the clock and start over.

In contrast, women who missed out on being "daddy's girl" may grow up believing they aren't appealing. The lack of attention and/or rejection of their feminine qualities and charms makes them feel unworthy of having that special spot in their father's life. The hunger for that prominent place in "daddy's world" pushes these young girls to become adept at taking care of household matters and providing day-to-day care for family members who need assistance with chores, shoulders to lean on, or someone to rely on during a crisis. Young women in these circumstances view their caring actions as a conduit for connection with loved ones and feel terrified when, later in life, their good deeds fail to attract and please their partners.

Having buried their longing for closeness to avoid the shame of feeling needy, these women crave the sense of connection that physical closeness brings and use their bodies as their primary source of intimacy. For them, sex in adulthood becomes the only safe and reliable way to get close without feeling ashamed. Providing sex for men under the guise of "caretaking" is an effective way of being wanted and desired without having to endure the shame of asking for it.

When a young woman views her neediness as something to guard against, she uses sex as an enticement, gratified that at least during the time of sexual intercourse, she has sole ownership of her man – he is literally inside her, filling her up with private, intimate parts of himself. She hates the moment when he withdraws after coitus, as if he is abandoning her, so she demands sex again soon after orgasm. Having her partner's sexual organ inside her is the only tangible proof that they have a special and exclusive bond. It's a "grown up" way of fulfilling the wish to be "daddy's little princess"; both parties are joined as one in a rapture that excludes everyone and everything else.

But while these women use sex to feel physically close, their male partners report feeling like studs in this scenario, rather than lovers sharing emotional and physical intimacy. Yearning to be seen in a more human way, these men attempt to perform well sexually to please their partners, hoping to get the tenderness of emotional intimacy as a reward. But often, the sexual act gets overlaid with stamina and endurance issues, proving prowess, and convincing the woman she is attractive and desirable. Sadly, her need to be cared for and loved as a person goes unmet.

When a man uses sex to connect with his partners, it may be a way of protesting against the lack of access to emotional intimacy through regular interaction. "Getting inside" the woman and having her "hold" and take in his most personal body parts may be a way of making her accept him intimately. Penetration and/or oral sex may give men some sense of power that they can get what they want – to open that door to the inner sanctum of a woman – because regardless of the amount or quality of sex with their partners, men seem much more distressed and unfulfilled by a cold and distant relationship than their wives.

In my practice, I've observed that men seek intimacy differently from women. While women feel comfortable and validated in seeking closeness through their sexuality, men hope their partner will sense their desire for emotional intimacy, so they don't have to risk feeling "needy." Yet all too often, the signals they put out are misread or ignored, so a man may resort to complaining about stress at work and his fears it will impact his health. This jumpstarts his spouse's maternal instinct, getting her to feel concerned and put him first – above children, household chores and other family duties. In this way, men can legitimize the quest for emotional connection by using fatigue, anxiety about climbing the career ladder, and overwhelm due to the responsibility of supporting a family (and extended family), to elicit care that preserves the masculine image, while avoiding the shame and humiliation of being vulnerable.

The temporary comfort that men and women get from sexual intercourse makes the times in between tense and interminable, yet often neither partner communicates the anxiety of wishing and hoping for the next burst of connection. Instead, it's channeled into doing things for one another, hoping for a reaction that makes them feel cherished and vital to their partner. If they were reared in families where physical caretaking actions were valued, the couple may escalate their caretaking behaviors. For example, they compensate for the lack of connection by developing a joint expertise in co-parenting and sharing household tasks. While this may work for a while, the breaking point comes when they stop resonating with each other's overtures and intentions, and each feels like they're busting a gut to make their love and commitment blip on their partner's radar.

When a couple reaches this impasse, often one partner will do something outside the marriage that brings this stalemate to a head. Wives may get involved in their career or child rearing, making their husbands feel even less wanted and important, or they may have a liaison outside the relationship. This cheating is often to satisfy the need for control in the marriage when caretaking and seduction have failed. Managing secret assignations to suit her schedule and being able to pick up and discard another man at whim provides a heady sense of power for a woman who is struggling with a relationship where there is increasing concern about the quality of intimacy.

When men cheat, in the majority of cases the main purpose is to force their partners to hear, soothe, and care for them, and above all to be elevated to the number one slot in the woman's life. I have found that, in many cases, it's a last-ditch attempt to show their wives how desperate they are for nurturing without asking for it in a way that shames them. Unfortunately, it has the opposite effect: Men are shut out of their primary relationship even more and deprived of the only closeness they did have – sexual intercourse. At this point, many men opt to continue their affairs to maintain some self-esteem through their mistresses, who no doubt are insatiable for time and contact with them. Just as women who cheat often enjoy the exhilaration of being in control, so men opt for the power of having an alternate woman who salivates at the sound of their voice. But deep inside, they want their partner to reclaim them and give them all the adoration and care that they get from their paramour.

If and when their female partners tune in to their emotional wounds, men feel wanted and loved, but all too often the women they're with feel they're taking care of a child, rather than a partner. The fear that they will not be satisfied emotionally makes them push their babyish men away, causing both partners to retreat to their respective corners, wary of trying to connect again.

The men who ask me to help save their marriages are committed to getting their emotional needs met by their wives and have no interest in substitutes. It becomes their mission in life to *make* their spouses give them what they missed out on as children, and what they are determined to get through the bonds of marriage. Generally, the wife has to make amends for the negligence of the mother. In these cases, she's less likely to want to attend therapy, believing that there is nothing in it for her.

But while couples counseling is the preferred and more accepted route to solving problems in a marriage, it isn't always necessary or effective. In cases where the partners are combative, each wanting validation for their perspective, couples therapy is unlikely to develop the empathy, acceptance and sense of equality that's the foundation for lasting emotional intimacy. Often, the most clients gain is short-term containment of overwhelming rivalry and temporary abatement of power struggles, as they play out their contentious relationship in front of the therapist, constantly switching between the roles of sadistic ogre and martyred victim.

In these cases, it's preferable and more productive to work with the partner who most wants the intimacy and connection – and that's usually the man. If that one partner is determined to save the relationship by unraveling the couple's destructive game plan, the marriage can thrive and offer both partners a comfortable and fulfilling emotional closeness. The bitter seeds that sprouted fear can be rescued from their barren soil and nurtured into receptive and giving humans, able to empathize, share, accept, tolerate and grow together through the storms of life.

Made in the USA
Lexington, KY
14 December 2018